React.js Crash Course:

Build Interactive UIs in Record Time

KRISTIAN B. SCHUSTER

Contents

Introduction: Welcome to the React.js Revolution – Build Interactive UIs, FAST!

So, you're ready to dive into React.js? Excellent! You've picked a great framework for building modern, interactive web interfaces. And you want to learn it quickly? Even better! This book is designed to get you coding real React applications in record time, skipping the unnecessary theory and focusing on practical skills.

Forget about wading through endless documentation or getting bogged down in complex configurations. This crash course will give you the essential knowledge and hands-on experience you need to start building amazing user interfaces with React.

Why React? Speed, Reusability, and the Component Model – The Power of Efficiency

React has taken the web development world by storm, and for good reason. Here's why React is such a popular and powerful choice:

Speed: React's virtual DOM and efficient rendering algorithms make it incredibly fast, resulting in smooth and responsive user interfaces.

Reusability: React's component-based architecture allows you to break down your UI into reusable building blocks, making your code more organized and maintainable.

Component Model: React allows you to build reusable UI components, making your code more organized and maintainable. Its well-defined component lifecycle makes it easier to manage the state and behavior of your components.

Declarative Programming: React encourages a declarative style of programming, where you describe what you want the UI to look like, and React handles the details of how to achieve it. This makes your code more readable and easier to reason about.

Large Community and Ecosystem: React has a large and active community, providing a wealth of resources, libraries, and tools to support your development efforts.

A Personal Insight: I was blown away by how quickly I could build complex UIs with React. The component-based architecture made it so much easier to manage and reuse code. It really changed the way I think about web development.

Who This Book Is For: The Ambitious Developer

This book is for developers who want to learn React.js quickly and efficiently. It's perfect for:

JavaScript Developers: Looking to add React to their skillset and build modern web applications.

Front-End Developers: Wanting to learn a popular and in-demand framework.

Full-Stack Developers: Aiming to build the user interfaces of their Javascript code and applications.

Developers with Some JavaScript Experience: Assumes basic knowledge of Javascript functions.

What You'll Build: Tangible Skills and a Portfolio Piece

Throughout this book, you'll learn by doing, building a series of practical mini-projects that will solidify your understanding of React concepts and give you a portfolio piece to showcase your skills. By the end of this book, you'll be able to build:

A Simple Todo App

A Basic Blog with Posts

An Interactive Quiz Application

An E-commerce Product Listing

A Weather App

And more!

Conventions Used: Getting the Most Out of This Book

To maximize your learning experience, we'll use the following conventions throughout this book:

Code Examples: Code examples will be presented in a clear and concise style, with comments to explain what each line of code does.

Step-by-Step Instructions: We'll break down complex tasks into smaller, more manageable steps.

Tips and Best Practices: We'll provide helpful tips and best practices to help you write more efficient and maintainable code.

Warnings and Cautions: We'll call out potential pitfalls and common mistakes to help you avoid errors.

Personal Insights: We'll share our own experiences and insights to make the learning process more engaging and relatable.

Chapter 1: Ignite Your React Skills: Setting Up and Seeing Results FAST – From Zero to React in Minutes!

Alright, enough talk – let's code! This chapter is all about getting your React development environment set up and displaying your first "Hello, World!" message in the browser. We're skipping the long explanations and getting straight to the action. Think of this as lighting the fuse on your React rocket ship.

By the end of this chapter, you'll have a working React application that you can start building upon. Let's get started!

1.1 Installing Node.js and npm (or yarn) – Powering Up Your JavaScript Backend

Alright, future Node.js masters! Before you can start building anything amazing, you need the right tools. Think of this as setting up your workshop, and the first thing you need is an engine and a toolbox! In this case, it's a Javascript engine and a package management system.

This section will walk you through installing Node.js (which includes npm) and give you a quick introduction to Yarn as an alternative package manager.

The Core: Node.js

Node.js is the JavaScript runtime environment that allows you to execute JavaScript code outside of a web browser. It's built on Chrome's V8 JavaScript engine and provides a powerful and efficient platform for building server-side applications.

1. **Head to the Source:** Navigate your browser to the URL.
2. **Pick LTS:** Select the version that has "LTS" or Long-Term Support.

A Personal Insight: It may be tempting to get the latest and greatest, but you are going to have to deal with headaches. It's a better long-term strategy to select the LTS.

1. **Run the Installer:** Double click the file, and follow the steps.
2. **Make sure you add to PATH**

This makes it easier to run.

1. **Check to see if it all works!**

To do so, open your terminal and run

```
node -v
```

and if you see the version numbers, then all is set!

The Power Tools: npm (Node Package Manager) and Yarn

Node.js has a useful command to manage the different Javascript code and packages.

These are the toolboxes that are used.

NPM or Node Package Manager comes with Node!

If you run

```
npm -v
```

And the version shows up, then congrats!

A Personal Insight: At this stage, I would recommend familiarizing yourself with the different NPM commands since the more you know the better!

The other popular alternative is yarn.

Here are the commands to install the yarn.

```
npm install --global yarn
```

1.2 Creating a package.json File: Managing Your Project's Identity and Dependencies

Alright, you've installed Node.js and npm (or yarn). Now, it's time to create a package.json file for your first Node.js project. This file is like a digital passport for your project, containing important metadata and managing its dependencies. Think of it as the central nervous system for your project. What does it do? It identifies the project, tracks the version, and lists all the different packages you have to download.

You can have a lot of different codes to play with, and if you want to use these for multiple different projects, it is key that you are able to keep it up.

This section will show you:

- What is package.json file?
- How to create the code?
- What to do with the dependencies?

Then you are ready to fly!

What is package.json? Project Identity and Dependency Manager

The package.json file is a JSON file that contains metadata about your project, including its name, version, description, entry point, scripts, dependencies, and more. It's essential for managing dependencies, publishing your project to npm, and automating various development tasks.

A Personal Insight: I think of the package.json file as the heart and soul of my Node.js project. It's the first file I create and the one I consult most frequently.

Creating a package.json File: Two Approaches

There are two main ways to create a package.json file:

1. **Using npm init (Interactive):** This is the most common and beginner-friendly approach. Simply run the command npm init in your project directory, and npm will guide you through a series of prompts, asking you for information about your project.
   2.   `npm init`

   You'll be asked questions like:

   - package name: (your-project-name)
   - version: (1.0.0)
   - description: (A brief description of your project)
   - entry point: (index.js)
   - test command: (leave blank for now)
   - git repository: (if you have one)
   - keywords: (a list of keywords)
   - author: (Your Name)
   - license: (ISC)

You can accept the default values by pressing Enter, or you can enter your own values.

3. **Using npm init -y (Automatic):** This creates a package.json file with default values, skipping all the prompts. This is useful for quickly creating a basic package.json file.

```
4.        npm init -y
```

You can then edit the file manually to customize the metadata.

Here's what a basic package.json file might look like:

```json
{
  "name": "my-nodejs-app",
  "version": "1.0.0",
  "description": "A simple Node.js application",
  "main": "index.js",
  "scripts": {
    "start": "node index.js"
  },
  "keywords": [],
  "author": "Your Name",
  "license": "ISC"
}
```

A Personal Insight: I almost always use npm init interactively, as it forces me to think about the key metadata for my project. However, npm init -y can be a useful shortcut for quickly creating a basic package.json file.

What About Dependencies? Listing Your Project's Needs

The most important part of the package.json file is the dependencies object. This object lists all the external packages that your project depends on.

To install a package and add it to your dependencies object, you can use the npm install command with the --save flag (or --save-dev for development dependencies):

```
npm install express --save
```

This will install the express package and add it to the dependencies object in your package.json file:

```json
{
  "dependencies": {
    "express": "^4.17.1"
  }
}
```

The ^4.17.1 specifies the version range for the express package. In this case, it means that npm will install any version of express that is compatible with version 4.17.1.

A Personal Insight: Always remember to save the dependencies so you can quickly install the code.

Conclusion: Your Project's Identity

By creating a package.json file, you've given your project a clear identity and established a mechanism for managing its dependencies. This is a crucial step in building maintainable and scalable Node.js applications.

1.3 Project Structure Essentials – The Lay of the Land: Setting Up for Success

You've installed Node.js and set up your package.json. You're about to dive into React code, but first, let's talk about organization. A well-structured project is easier to navigate, maintain, and collaborate on. Think of this as laying the foundation for a well-organized home – knowing where everything goes makes life so much easier!

This section will cover:

- The rationale behind having a good project structure.
- The files and directories that come with Create React App.
- Recommended folder structures for larger projects.

Why Project Structure Matters: Order from Chaos

Before we dive into code, it's important to understand *why* project structure is important. A well-organized project makes it easier to:

- **Find Files Quickly:** No more hunting through a disorganized mess to find the component you need.
- **Understand the Codebase:** A clear structure makes it easier to understand how different parts of the application relate to each other.
- **Maintain and Update Code:** A well-organized codebase is easier to modify and update, reducing the risk of introducing bugs.
- **Collaborate with Others:** A consistent structure makes it easier for team members to work together effectively.

A Personal Insight: I've worked on projects with terrible project structures, and it's a nightmare. It's like trying to find a specific grain of sand on a beach. Spending a little time upfront to create a good structure will save you countless hours down the road.

The Create React App Structure: A Solid Starting Point

Create React App (CRA) provides a sensible default project structure that's perfect for getting started with React. Here's a breakdown of the key files and directories:

- **node_modules/:** This directory contains all the npm packages that your project depends on. *Don't* modify anything in this directory directly.
- **public/:** This directory contains static assets, such as HTML files, images, and fonts.
  - index.html: The main HTML file for your application. This is where your React app will be rendered.
- **src/:** This is where most of your React code will live.
  - App.js: The main component of your application. This is where you'll start building your UI.
  - index.js: The entry point for your React application. This is where you'll render the App component into the DOM.
  - index.css: The main CSS file for your application.
  - App.css: The CSS file specifically for the App component.
  - App.test.js: A file for writing unit tests for the App component.
  - logo.svg: The React logo.
- **package.json:** This file contains metadata about your project, including its name, version, dependencies, and scripts.
- **.gitignore:** This file specifies which files and directories should be ignored by Git.

A Personal Insight: The src/ directory is where you'll spend most of your time as a React developer. Getting familiar with its structure is key to navigating your codebase effectively.

Scaling Up: Recommended Folder Structures for Larger Projects

As your React application grows, you may want to adopt a more structured folder organization within the src/ directory. Here are a few common approaches:

- **Feature-Based Structure:** Group files by feature (e.g., src/components/UserProfile/, src/components/ProductList/). This is a good approach for applications with clear feature boundaries.
- **Type-Based Structure:** Group files by type (e.g., src/components/, src/hooks/, src/utils/). This is a good approach for applications with a large number of components or a complex data flow.
- **Atomic Design:** A methodology for designing UI systems that breaks down components into smaller, reusable units (Atoms, Molecules, Organisms, Templates, Pages).

Here's an example of a feature-based structure:

```
    src/
components/
  UserProfile/
    UserProfile.js
    UserProfile.css
    UserProfile.test.js
  ProductList/
    ProductList.js
    ProductList.css
    ProductList.test.js
services/ # For API calls
```

```
    api.js
  utils/ # Helper functions
    formatDate.js
  App.js
  index.js
```

A Personal Insight: I've found that a feature-based structure works best for most of my React projects. It makes it easy to find all the files related to a specific feature and to reason about the code.

Conclusion: A Foundation for Growth

By understanding the essential elements of React project structure, you're setting yourself up for success. A well-organized codebase is easier to navigate, maintain, and collaborate on. And as your applications grow in complexity, a solid foundation will be more important than ever.

Let's move on and write some code.

1.4 Your First Component: "Hello, World!" – Let's Build Something!

You've set up your project structure, and now it's time to write some React code! The core of React development is the concept of *components*. Think of components as reusable building blocks that you can use to create your user interface. They're like LEGO bricks that you can snap together to build complex structures.

In this section, we'll create your first React component: the classic "Hello, World!" example. This will give you a taste of what React development is like and introduce you to the essential concepts of JSX and rendering.

What is a Component? The Building Block of React

A React component is a self-contained unit of code that renders a specific part of the user interface. Components can be simple, like a button or a text label, or complex, like an entire page or form. You can compose a lot of these to create a bigger code.

Key characteristics of a React component:

- **Reusable:** You can use the same component multiple times in your application.
- **Composable:** You can combine smaller components to create larger components.
- **Maintainable:** Components are self-contained, making them easier to update and debug.

A Personal Insight: Thinking in terms of components is key to mastering React. It's about breaking down your UI into manageable pieces and then building them up into a cohesive whole.

Functional Components: The Modern Approach

There are two main types of React components: class components and functional components. In modern React development, functional components are preferred because they are simpler, more concise, and easier to test. They also work seamlessly with React Hooks (which we'll cover later).

A functional component is simply a JavaScript function that returns JSX (more on that in the next section).

Let's start with this base

```
    function MyComponent() {
  return (
    <div>
      {/* JSX code goes here */}
    </div>
  );
}

export default MyComponent;
```

You are now starting to get into Javascript!

- **function MyComponent() { ... }:** This defines a JavaScript function called MyComponent. This is your React component.
- **return (...):** This tells the component to output something! It will return the JSX that will be rendered to the DOM.

JSX: Writing HTML-like Code in JavaScript

JSX (JavaScript XML) is a syntax extension to JavaScript that allows you to write HTML-like code within your JavaScript files. It makes it easier to create and manipulate HTML elements dynamically.

Here's an example of JSX:

```
    const name = "Alice";
const element = <h1>Hello, {name}!</h1>;
```

This code creates a React element that displays the text "Hello, Alice!". The curly braces {} are used to embed JavaScript expressions within the JSX.

A Personal Insight: JSX can be a bit strange at first, but once you get used to it, it becomes incredibly natural and intuitive. It's like writing HTML with the power of JavaScript at your fingertips.

Creating the "Hello, World!" Component

Let's put it all together and create your first React component:

```
// src/components/HelloWorld.js

import React from 'react';

function HelloWorld() {
  return (
    <h1>Hello, World!</h1>
  );
}

export default HelloWorld;
```

Let's break down what each part does:

1. *Import React*: You need to include the line that imports the Javascript and React library in order to make this all work.
2. *Create the arrow function*
3. *Create the return*
4. *Export*: You want all the code to go out and be useful!

To call it all, you still need to put the code in app.js.

The React App
Now you need to put it all into the main app! So first import!

```
import HelloWorld from './components/HelloWorld';
```

And then to run it!

```
function App() {
  return (
    <div className="App">
      <HelloWorld />
    </div>
  );
}
```

That's all it takes!

A Personal Insight: Do not worry about why this is. We will cover all of that in more detail in the next sections!

You Have Unlocked The Power!
So now you've done it! You are now able to take the code and have it be run. This is what you will need to proceed.

1.5 Running Your React App – Seeing Your Creation in Action

You've created your first component, and now it's time for the moment of truth: seeing it in action! Running your React app is easy with Create React App. Think of this as launching your ship and setting sail!

In this section, we'll cover how to start the development server, view your application in the browser, and understand the basics of the development environment.

The Magic Command: npm start

To start your React application, simply open the command prompt or terminal, navigate to your project directory, and type the following command:

```
npm start
```

This command uses the start script that's defined in your package.json file. Create React App automatically configures this script to start a development server that will:

- Serve your React application in the browser.
- Automatically reload the page when you make changes to your code.
- Provide helpful error messages in the console.

After running npm start, you should see a message in the console that tells you the address of your React application. It's typically http://localhost:3000.

Viewing Your Application in the Browser: Your Window to the World

Open your web browser and navigate to the address that was printed in the console (usually http://localhost:3000). You should see your React application running! If you followed the "Hello, World!" example from the previous section, you should see the text "Hello, World!" displayed on the page.

If you make any changes to your React code, the browser will automatically reload, and you'll see the changes reflected in the page. This is because Create React App includes a "hot reloading" feature that makes development much faster and more efficient.

A Personal Insight: The first time I saw hot reloading in action, I was amazed. It was like having a superpower – the ability to see my code changes instantly reflected in the browser without having to manually refresh the page.

Understanding the Development Environment: Your Coding Workshop

When you run npm start, Create React App sets up a development environment that is optimized for local development. This environment includes:

- **A Development Server:** This serves your React application and provides hot reloading.
- **Webpack:** A module bundler that packages your JavaScript, CSS, and other assets into optimized bundles for deployment.
- **Babel:** A JavaScript compiler that transforms modern JavaScript syntax (ES6+) into code that can be run in older browsers.
- **ESLint:** A linter that helps you identify and fix coding style issues.

You don't need to understand all the details of these tools to get started with React. Create React App handles most of the configuration for you, allowing you to focus on writing code.

A Personal Insight: As you become more experienced with React, you may want to customize the default Create React App configuration. There are tools you can use to customize, but I recommend reading the documentation first and understanding the trade-offs involved.

Congratulations! You've taken the first step.

You've successfully set up your development environment, created your first React component, and run your React application in the browser. You're now ready to dive deeper into the world of React and start building more complex and interactive user interfaces.

Chapter 2: Components: The Building Blocks of React – Mastering Reusability

You've got React running! Now you have to take it to the next level!

This section is all about learning how to code with Javascript with the key concept of Javascript and React: Components. Think of React components as pre-fabricated sections of code that can be reused to make that code all that much better.

In this chapter, we'll explore the world of React components! And we will learn about:

*Different Kinds of Components

*JSX: Building Components

*Passing Data to Components

*Styling Components

2.1 Functional vs. Class Components: A Quick Comparison – Choosing Your Style

You now know how to make components! But what does the best component do? Well, there are all kinds of new Javascript techniques that you can use, but you need to know what is best for you!

In React, there are two primary types of components: functional components and class components. While both can be used to create user interfaces, they have different characteristics and are suited for different situations. It is important to consider what can best fit the style that you want and to what needs that you may have.

In this section, we'll explore:

*What are the core differences?
*Why has there been a shift?
*A recommendation on what to do.

Let's dive in!

Functional Components: Simple and Concise

Functional components are, at their core, Javascript functions! They use the command with an arrow. They are very basic!

For example

```
    const MyComponent = () => {
  return (
    <div>
      <h1>Hello from a functional component!</h1>
    </div>
  );
};
```

These are very simple to understand, and you can put it all together to then help implement what you need.

A Personal Insight: I really love these! They are so much easier to use and they are so easy for what I want to do.

Class Components: A More Historical Approach

Class components are created using ES6 classes, which is why it is very important to learn Javascript!

```
    class MyComponent extends React.Component {
  render() {
    return (
      <div>
        <h1>Hello from a class component!</h1>
      </div>
    );
  }
}
```

There is a lot more code, it can be more challenging to read, but it is more powerful! Before the advent of React Hooks (we'll touch on these later), class components were the *only* way to manage state and perform side effects.

So, why would anyone use it?

- You have to use it to convert old code.
- You want to do something unique!

2.2 Creating Functional Components – Your First Component

You now know the different parts of a Javascript component, with all the different pros and cons! Now, we'll focus on the modern and more preferred method, which is to create your first real Javascript code. What is so great is how little code it actually takes to make something that means something.

What will be in this version?

*The Base Code
*How to Make It Adapt to Different Changes.
*What next?

Let's get started.

The Base Code

All of it starts with these lines of code. You can then use it to create the base for all that you want.

```
import React from 'react';

function MyComponent() {
  return (
    <div>
      <h1>Hello, world!</h1>
    </div>
  );
}

export default MyComponent;
```

What does that actually mean?

To understand this, let's break it down!

- import React from 'react'; This is needed to use React.
- function MyComponent() { ... } This defines your component. The component's name should always start with a capital letter.
- return (...) This will display the code that you want.
- export default MyComponent; This is what allows it all to work.

How to Make It Adapt to Different Changes

To make it more dynamic, it is very common to call it with what is known as *props*.

To do this, you would change it to:

```
    import React from 'react';

function MyComponent(props) {
  return (
    <div>
      <h1>Hello, {props.name}!</h1>
    </div>
  );
}

export default MyComponent;
```

"Props" is short for properties.

A Personal Insight: You might as well get used to copying and pasting this in everything! At first, it may be difficult, but you will then be used to it.

In short

You have a container, all you have to do is to keep it in order, and to make sure you have all the right pieces! And that is what makes Javascript so great. So good luck!

2.3 JSX: Writing HTML-like Code in JavaScript – Bridging the Worlds of Structure and Logic

You now have the structure of Javascript to build your code. Then, you have to think about what the user sees. Is there a way to do both in the same place? You bet there is!

JSX is a syntax extension to JavaScript that allows you to write HTML-like code within your JavaScript files. Think of it as a bridge between the worlds of structure (HTML) and logic (JavaScript), allowing you to create dynamic and interactive user interfaces with ease.

It is a tool that helps unlock the power of Javascript!

This section will help you:

- What is JSX?
- JSX != HTML
- Javascript in JSX!

What is JSX? It's HTML... But Not Quite

JSX stands for JavaScript XML. You will see a lot of examples that show very similar code but it is not!

```
    const element = <h1>Hello, world!</h1>;
```

That looks a lot like HTML, but it's actually Javascript! The purpose of JSX is to make it easier to write Javascript code!

A Personal Insight: When I started, I would often think that it was just HTML, and it took some time to realize what I was doing!

To make it JSX, here are the requirements!

- Must return a single root element.
- Use className instead of class.
- Use camelCase for HTML attributes.

Let's dive in and see what this means.

- **Single Root Element:**

In JSX, a component must return a single root element. This means that all of your HTML-like code must be wrapped inside a single parent element.

This is correct!

```
    // Valid JSX
<div>
  <h1>Hello, world!</h1>
  <p>This is a paragraph.</p>
</div>
```

This is not!

```
    // Invalid JSX (multiple root elements)
<h1>Hello, world!</h1>
<p>This is a paragraph.</p>
```

- **className instead of class:**

The class attribute is a reserved keyword in JavaScript, so JSX uses className instead.

```
    <div className="my-class">This is a div with a class.</div>
```

- **Camel Case:**

It is the format that we have talked about before.

A Personal Insight: The great part is that the error messages in Javascript are very descriptive. So if you forget, it will help remind you!

Javascript in JSX

You can also embed Javascript in JSX. But it's important to know how it's all done!

To do so, use curly braces!

```
const name = "Alice";
const element = <h1>Hello, {name}!</h1>;
```

You can also use this for different functions!

```
function formatName(user) {
  return user.firstName + ' ' + user.lastName;
}

const user = {
  firstName: 'Harper',
  lastName: 'Perez'
};

const element = (
  <h1>
    Hello, {formatName(user)}!
  </h1>
);
```

With all those tools, you are now able to bring Javascript and HTML together to do all that you wanted to do. It's time to see what more you can do to unleash the power of Javascript!

Okay, let's craft an engaging and practical section 2.4, "Props: Passing Data to Components," designed to illuminate how to make your components dynamic and reusable by passing data to them.

2.4 Props: Passing Data to Components – Giving Components Instructions

You now know how to create basic HTML. But what to do? How to have that data shown? That is the purpose of Props in Javascript - it's short for properties! With it, you can customize how it will show up!

Think of it as how you can make an amazing code that follows Javascript and that all you have to do is change the input, like an amazing machine!

In this section, we'll explore how to pass data to components using props and how to use that data to render dynamic content.

What we will address:
*The theory of props

*How Javascript code implements props
*How to create the code to pass props!

What are Props?

Props are attributes that you can pass to a React component. They allow you to customize the behavior and appearance of the component.

A Personal Insight: You have to be very clear of what the Props are so that you are able to effectively get the data running! If not, then it is not a good use!

How to pass props?

First you must say what the components are!

```
function Welcome(props) {
  return <h1>Hello, {props.name}</h1>;
}
```

Then, you can use it to give the value!

```
function App() {
  return (
    <div>
      <Welcome name="Alice" />
      <Welcome name="Bob" />
    </div>
  );
}
```

What will that display?

```
Hello, Alice
Hello, Bob
```

And it works! It really is that simple.

A Personal Insight: For me, it took a while to get used to. But it's really about thinking what you want to pass, and what you want to get.

2.5 Styling Components: Inline Styles, CSS Classes, and CSS Modules – Making It Look Good

You've got the Javascript code to do what you want and you know how to pass it to other components! Now comes the next challenge! You have to actually make the webpage useful and have people look at it. To do that, you need to understand the art of styling!

To do that, there are different methods and the code that you will have to consider. So let's dive into the what and why.

What will be covered:
*In-line Styles
*CSS
*CSS Modules

A Personal Insight: I was always told that the art of coding is about making things work, but I disagree. The great coders are the ones that make it look good!

Inline Styles: What you can do to make the CSS code work. What can you do to make the HTML say what you want it to say?

To start, you can just put it all in one line.

```
    const MyComponent = () => {
  return (
    <div style={{ backgroundColor: 'lightblue', padding: '10px' }}>
      <h1>Hello, world!</h1>
    </div>
  );
};
```

That is it! However, you can't do all the things, it is more difficult to make code that is adaptive, and it is hard to have it look good.

A Personal Insight: I see this as a first step! Getting used to what kind of styles you want, and from there, you can build upon that.

CSS Styles: A Bit More Advanced

Instead of having all the different pieces and parts all in one, you can keep the CSS structure in an outside code and then put it in there!

To do this, you do this in your CSS file:

```
    .my-component {
  background-color: lightblue;
  padding: 10px;
}
```

Then, Javascript can see it with the command className!

```
    const MyComponent = () => {
  return (
    <div className="my-component">
      <h1>Hello, world!</h1>
```

```
    </div>
  );
};
```

A Personal Insight: I would say to always get it to work, and then to make it pretty later.

To put it all together, and to see what it does, what do we have?

Well, with what you have, it all can then be used to make some amazing things. What are you going to do with this information?

Chapter 3: State: Making Components Dynamic – Reacting to Change

Okay, so you have components! That's great! But what if nothing changes and the user just sees the same things all the time? That makes for a boring webpage! Now, let's get to state! Think of state as the memory of a component, allowing it to remember information and react to changes.

In essence, this will now make all the code that you have previously seen now be dynamic and make it so that it can run and be different!

In this section, we will be covering:

What is State?

Using the useState Hook: Managing Component State

Updating State: Triggers and Re-renders

Handling Events: Responding to User Actions

Controlled Components: Managing Form Input

These are all essential to making your app come to life so let's get started!

3.1 What is State? Your Component's Memory – Giving Your UI a Mind of Its Own

You've learned how to create components, but now how can you make them dynamic? How can you make it remember what the user has done? The key to that is *state*.

State is what allows React components to be interactive and dynamic. Think of state as a component's memory, where it stores information that can change over time and affect what is displayed on the screen.

So what does this mean? Well, what if we had an example without the state and with the state?

A Personal Insight: Before I had the ability to use state and to make my website "remember" what had been done, it was really hard! But with this, it opens up a whole new world!

Let's say you want to make Javascript code to keep track of the number of clicks on a button.

- **Without State**

You can only click the button, but what does it do? Nothing really.

- **With State**

To implement

1. You are going to make a state for the number.
2. Make a button.
3. Then, on every click, increase the state.

Here is the code:

```
import React, { useState } from 'react';

function MyComponent() {
  const [count, setCount] = useState(0);

  const handleClick = () => {
    setCount(count + 1);
  };

  return (
    <div>
      <p>You clicked {count} times</p>
      <button onClick={handleClick}>Click me</button>
    </div>
  );
}

export default MyComponent;
```

Every time you click, a higher number comes!

A Personal Insight: There is a lot that comes from this code, and if you can understand it, you will see how the different parts actually combine and you will be very good at coding in Javascript.

What are React Hooks?

It might be a good idea to talk about hooks! React Hooks are functions that let you "hook into" React state and lifecycle features from functional components. Hooks don't work inside classes - they let you use React without classes.

This is required to keep track of what has happened and to build out the best kind of Javascript.

3.2 Using the useState Hook: Managing Component State – Giving Your Components a Memory

You now know what state is and why it's important. But how do you actually *use* state in your React components? That's where the useState Hook comes in. Think of useState as a magic tool that allows you to add state to your functional components and update it whenever you need to.

This section will cover:

*What it does
*How to implement it
*What to think about when managing state.

Let's dive in!

What is the useState Hook?

The useState Hook is a built-in React Hook that allows you to add state to functional components. It returns an array with two elements:

1. **The current state value:** This is the current value of the state variable.
2. **A function to update the state:** This function allows you to update the value of the state variable and trigger a re-render of the component.

To use the useState Hook, you need to import it from the react library:

```
import React, { useState } from 'react';
```

How to Implement It

Here's how to use the useState Hook in a functional component:

```
function MyComponent() {
  const [count, setCount] = useState(0);

  // ...
}
```

Let's break this down:

1. const [count, setCount] = useState(0); This line declares a new state variable called count and initializes it to 0. It also declares a function called setCount that you can use to update the value of count. This uses array destructuring to assign the two returned values to variables.
2. The value inside of the function of useState is the default. In this case, the count will start at 0.

3. The two variables, count and setCount will now be what you use to refer to and change.

Here's an example:

```
import React, { useState } from 'react';

function MyComponent() {
  const [count, setCount] = useState(0);

  const handleClick = () => {
    setCount(count + 1);
  };

  return (
    <div>
      <p>You clicked {count} times</p>
      <button onClick={handleClick}>Click me</button>
    </div>
  );
}

export default MyComponent;
```

Now, let's go through it line by line!

1. To create some action, we have to set up a function.
2. Then, the value of the button is set to the function.
3. When you click the button, the number is changed.

And those are all the steps! With this, the code is ready to be shown and it will now function!

A Personal Insight: There's a lot to remember there, but after you write it a few times, it gets easier and easier! Then you can start to make it all yours!

What to Think About When Managing State: Immutability

In React, it's very important to treat state as immutable. This means that you should never directly modify the state variable. Instead, you should always use the update function (e.g., setCount) to update the state.

For example, don't do this:

```
// Incorrect (Directly Modifying State)
count = count + 1;
```

Instead, always use the update function:

```
// Correct (Using the Update Function)
setCount(count + 1);
```

A Personal Insight: Treating state as immutable is a key principle of React development. It helps to prevent unexpected side effects and makes your code easier to reason about and debug. It's worth the effort to get this right from the start.

Also, when updating objects, the way to do it is also with a slightly different code. Here's how you do it:

```
const [user, setUser] = useState({ name: 'Alice', age: 30 });

const updateName = () => {
  setUser({ ...user, name: 'Bob' });
};
```

What you are doing is:
Copying the other values over and then changing what is there.

3.3 Updating State: Triggers and Re-renders – Making the Magic Happen

You now know how to use the useState Hook to declare state variables in your functional components. But the real power of state comes from the ability to *update* those variables and trigger a re-render of the component, causing the user interface to reflect the new data.

Think of state updates as the fuel that drives the React engine. They are the events that trigger the component to recalculate what it should display and to update the DOM accordingly.

In this section, we'll explore how to update state variables using the update function provided by the useState Hook, and how those updates trigger re-renders.

What will we cover?

- The Role of State Update Functions
- How to Invoke it to trigger Re-renders
- Asynchronous State Updates

The Role of State Update Functions: The Correct Way to Change State

As we discussed before, it's crucial to treat state as immutable. You should *never* directly modify a state variable. Instead, you should always use the update function that is returned by the useState Hook.

For example, if you have a state variable called count, don't do this:

```
// Incorrect (Directly Modifying State)
count = count + 1; //Don't do it!
```

Instead, use the setCount function:
```
// Correct (Using the Update Function)
```

```
setCount(count + 1);
```

The update function is responsible for notifying React that the state has changed and that the component needs to be re-rendered.

Triggering Re-Renders: The React Engine in Action

When you call a state update function (e.g., setCount), React does the following:

1. **Schedules a Re-render:** React marks the component as "dirty," indicating that it needs to be re-rendered.
2. **Calculates the New UI:** React compares the new state with the previous state and determines which parts of the DOM need to be updated. This is done efficiently using a virtual DOM.
3. **Updates the DOM:** React applies the necessary changes to the actual DOM, updating the user interface to reflect the new state.

This process is highly optimized, ensuring that only the parts of the DOM that have actually changed are updated, minimizing the performance impact.

A Personal Insight: I used to wonder why React insisted on using update functions instead of allowing direct modification of state. But after I started working on larger and more complex applications, I realized how important it is for maintaining performance and predictability.

Asynchronous State Updates: Handling Dependencies

Sometimes, you may need to update state based on the previous value of the state. In these cases, it's important to use the functional form of the update function, which takes a function as an argument.

For example, instead of doing this:

```
    const handleClick = () => {
  setCount(count + 1); // Might not be accurate
};
```

You should do this:

```
    const handleClick = () => {
  setCount(prevCount => prevCount + 1); // Guarantees accuracy
};
```

The functional form of the update function guarantees that you're working with the most up-to-date value of the state, even if multiple updates are scheduled in quick succession.

A Personal Insight: I've encountered subtle bugs caused by not using the functional form of the update function. It's a good habit to always use it when updating state based on its previous value.

Conclusion: The Heartbeat of Your React Components

By mastering the art of updating state and understanding how those updates trigger re-renders, you'll be able to create truly dynamic and interactive React components. The most important thing is to keep in mind how the data is traveling and that you now know how to make it happen!

3.4 Handling Events: Responding to User Actions – Making Your Components Interactive

You now know how to change the state of the Javascript. That's only step one! What is next is to actually handle *events*, which is what the user is doing to make your function run!

In this section, we'll explore how to use event handlers to respond to user interactions, such as clicks, form submissions, and mouse movements.

Now, let's talk about the three phases!

- What is a function that handles it?
- How can you implement it all?
- What to do with the code?

What are Events? Javascript's Actions

Events are actions or occurrences that happen in the browser, such as a user clicking a button, hovering over an element, submitting a form, or loading a page. JavaScript allows you to listen for these events and execute specific code in response.

In React, you handle events by attaching *event handlers* to your components. An event handler is a function that is executed when a particular event occurs on a specific element.

Attaching Event Handlers: Connecting Actions to Code

To attach an event handler to an element in React, you use the on<EventName> attribute, where <EventName> is the name of the event you want to listen for (e.g., onClick, onSubmit, onMouseOver). You then assign the event handler function to this attribute.

```
    function MyComponent() {
  const handleClick = () => {
    console.log("Button clicked!");
  };

  return (
```

```
    <button onClick={handleClick}>Click me</button>
  );
}
```

In this example, the onClick attribute is used to attach the handleClick function to the button element. When the button is clicked, the handleClick function will be executed, and the message "Button clicked!" will be logged to the console.

A Personal Insight: This can be tricky! For me, I used to get confused if the quotation marks were inside the Javascript, or outside.

Accessing Event Data: What Did the User Do?

When an event occurs, React passes an *event object* to the event handler function. This object contains information about the event, such as the target element, the type of event, and any data associated with the event.

To access the event object, you simply include it as the first argument to your event handler function:

```
    function MyComponent() {
  const handleClick = (event) => {
    console.log("Event type:", event.type); // Output: Event type: click
    console.log("Target element:", event.target); // Output: The Button
  };

  return (
    <button onClick={handleClick}>Click me</button>
  );
}
```

With this, you can now see what is all happening and know how to test for all of the information.

What are the different types of events?
There are a ton of different kinds that you can use, here are a few!

- onClick:

This is one of the most common events as it is a button!

- onChange:

This is also a common event! What can you do? This is whenever the input changes.

- onSubmit:

And finally, what about when submitting the code?

A Personal Insight: It takes a lot of time to get the different codes to what they are supposed to do! So take your time and remember to try and test all of the code!

3.5 Controlled Components: Managing Form Input – Taking Control of Your Forms

You now know about all these events and actions in Javascript! But what about Javascript forms? In particular, how can we use Javascript to control the HTML form?
What is the key to doing this? You need to make sure that the HTML form is connected to the Javascript!

This chapter will discuss how the user data flows and how the Javascript code can be used to make it all work.

We Will Discuss:
*Uncontrolled Components
*Controlled Components:
*Connecting it all!

It is all about what you want and getting to the point where the users are actually using it.

What Are Uncontrolled Components

To understand why controlled components are the best choice, it is important to know what the other style is.

With uncontrolled components, the values of what the user inputs are actually kept in the DOM.

You don't even need to use Javascript!

```
    <form>
  <label>
    Name:
    <input type="text" name="name" />
  </label>
  <button type="submit">Submit</button>
</form>
```

This can be good since there is very little code and you can just use it.

A Personal Insight: I have found that uncontrolled components are good for just gathering information to send to a server, for example, to sign up for a newsletter.

Controlled Components: The React Way

In React, the recommended approach is to use *controlled components*. With controlled components, the value of the input element is controlled by the React component's state. This gives you complete control over the form data and allows you to perform validation and other operations on the data as the user types.

A Personal Insight: At first, this seems to be more code for the same result. But after a while, you will find that if you are doing anything remotely complicated, that this structure is essential to making the whole project work.

Connecting it All

1. Create a state with useState to track the value.
2. Create a function to change the state every time it is changed.
3. Make sure to connect the value to the input!
4. ???
5. Profit!

Okay, maybe we should just put down some code instead. To start, here is the HTML portion of the code.

```
<input type="text" value={this.state.value}
onChange={this.handleChange} />
```

Here is the Javascript portion of the code.

```
constructor(props) {
super(props);
this.state = {value: ''};

this.handleChange = this.handleChange.bind(this);
this.handleSubmit = this.handleSubmit.bind(this);
}
```

To explain,

*   value references the state of the item.
*   handleChange is the code that is called to update the state for the value.

A Personal Insight: I have found that this setup can be quite a lot of code to do. It's helpful to just copy and paste, then modify the specific variables to what you need.

Chapter 4: Lists and Keys: Rendering Dynamic Data – Making Your Data Shine

Okay, you've learned how to make dynamic code that can change. What about having a list? That requires some thought because having a long list of names, or a list of images, or even code, can be a nightmare. It needs to be organized. That is what this chapter is about!

In this chapter, we'll explore how to render lists of data in React using Javascript. We'll learn about the importance of keys, how to map data to components, and how to filter and sort data.

What This Section Will Cover

*Rendering Lists

*Why You Need Keys?

*Mapping Data to Components

*Filtering and Sorting

You have now unlocked all the Javascript to make that code work. Is this what it means to have Javascript? Let's find out!

4.1 Rendering Lists of Data – From Data to UI: Bringing Your Data to Life

You now know all the methods of making and changing it! Now it's time to present the Javascript to the world. Here is how you can do so.

Rendering lists of data is a common task in web development. Whether you're displaying a list of products, a list of users, or a list of articles, you'll need to know how to efficiently render that data in your user interface.

That's what this section will show:
*How to take Javascript and add it to your code,
*Show different tricks and tools that can be used to make it easier for you to code,
*Show all the different ways that I think you can get the most value from the implementation of Javascript code!

A Personal Insight: It can be frustrating to manually create all the HTML for it, so it's a great feeling once you get this code working.

The key is the map() function, which is the key to making this all work.

The .map() function is a core Javascript function that does that! It takes the array and applies the code to each element.

Here is an example,

```
const numbers = [1, 2, 3, 4, 5];

const doubledNumbers = numbers.map(number => number * 2);

console.log(doubledNumbers); // Output: [2, 4, 6, 8, 10]
```

It might be hard to see how this is helpful! But it will be! Let's say you have a bunch of data, and you want all of them to be in a specific format:

```
const items = [
  { id: 1, name: 'Apple', price: 0.99 },
  { id: 2, name: 'Banana', price: 0.59 },
  { id: 3, name: 'Orange', price: 0.79 }
];
const itemList = items.map(item => (
  <li key={item.id}>
    {item.name} - ${item.price}
  </li>
));
```

What is happening with this code:

1. items.map Is a way to access each element of Javascript.
2. Then, the function that is called is used to create the HTML element.

A Personal Insight: After all of that, what's important is to see that you are creating more HTML code based on the values that you have created!

What if you do not have a key?

There will be times, such as getting basic data that you do not have a key that is passed along. In those cases, you can use the index!

```
const items = ['Apple', 'Banana', 'Orange'];
const itemList = items.map((item, index) => (
  <li key={index}>
    {item}
  </li>
```

```
));
```

What comes next is that you need to keep track of that code! So that is why I highly recommend that you do what is needed to keep track. This then helps make all Javascript code that much easier!

4.2 The Importance of Keys – Helping React Keep Track

You now know the methods to help create and manage lists of data and show them to your users! But what if you make changes? Javascript needs a way to keep track of this and a way to make sure that things don't get mixed up. Keys are what that is!

Think of keys as unique identifiers for each item in a list, allowing React to efficiently update the DOM when the list changes. Without keys, React has to re-render the entire list every time an item is added, removed, or reordered, which can lead to performance issues, especially for large lists.

Why is this important? What are the benefits?

What you need to understand is:

*Why Javascript keys are important,
*How to use them and to avoid problems, and
*What best practices you should follow.

With that, let's get on this journey!

The Problem: Without Keys, It's All Guesswork

Let's say you have a list of items you are displaying on the screen. It is all working well and good. But you want to add more items to the list. Then, Javascript can't know which one you are changing!

To illustrate, here is what happens if you did not have a key.

```
    <ul>
  <li>Item 1</li>
  <li>Item 2</li>
</ul>
```

If you now added an item to the list. The Javascript code would have to re-render all of the items!

A Personal Insight: There can be a performance hit on your code if you don't use keys!

Keys: Giving React a Helping Hand

To help React keep track of the items in the list, you can provide a key prop to each element. The key should be a unique identifier that distinguishes that element from other elements in the list.

The key helps Javascript identify it. Let's modify the previous example to include keys:

```
    <ul>
  <li key="1">Item 1</li>
  <li key="2">Item 2</li>
</ul>
```

Now, if you insert a new item with key="0" at the beginning of the list, React can efficiently update the DOM by only adding the new item, without re-rendering the existing items.

A Personal Insight: I have learned that this has to be a constant! Otherwise, it defeats the purpose!

Using Keys Effectively: Best Practices

Here are some best practices for using keys:

- **Use Unique and Stable Keys:** Keys should be unique and stable across re-renders. This means that the key for a particular item should not change unless the item itself is being replaced.
- **Use Data from Your Data Source:** The best keys are typically derived from your data source, such as a unique ID from a database.
- **Avoid Using Array Indices as Keys (Unless Absolutely Necessary):** Using array indices as keys can lead to performance problems, especially when the list is reordered.

A Personal Insight: It's really easy to just use the array indices, but it can cause more problems than it is worth!

4.3 Mapping Data to Components – Building Reusable Structures

You've mastered the fundamentals of Javascript arrays and you've mastered the use of keys! It all comes together when you use the .map() command to make every part of your code come to life. The key is to take those basic components and to make them work all over the Javascript program!

In this section, we'll explore how to use the .map() method to transform data and render it.

What do you need to do to get there?

1. Use .map()
2. All you need to know to use it effectively!

The Power of .map(): Transforming Data into UI

At the heart of rendering data is the map() method, which is available on all Javascript arrays. The map() method takes a function as an argument and applies that function to each element in the array, returning a *new* array with the transformed values.

The basic syntax is:

```
const newData = originalArray.map(item => {
// Perform transformation on item
return transformedItem;
});
```

A Personal Insight: I like to think of map() as a magical conveyor belt. You put your original data on one end, and it comes out the other end transformed into something you can display in your UI.

Putting It All Together: A List of Items

Let's say you have an array of product objects:

```
const products = [
{ id: 1, name: 'Laptop', price: 1200 },
{ id: 2, name: 'Keyboard', price: 75 },
{ id: 3, name: 'Mouse', price: 25 }
];
```

You can use the map() method to transform this array into an array of JSX elements that can be rendered in your component:

```
function ProductList({ products }) {
return (
  <ul>
    {products.map(product => (
      <li key={product.id}>
        {product.name} - ${product.price}
      </li>
    ))}
  </ul>
);
}
```

Here's a breakdown of what's happening:

1. {products.map(product => (...))}: This is where the magic happens. The map() method iterates over each product in the products array.
2. <li key={product.id}>: Each product is transformed into an <li> element. The key prop is set to the product.id, which is essential for React to efficiently update the list.

3. {item.name} - ${item.price}: This displays the name and price of the product within the <li> element.

A Personal Insight: At this point, you may ask what the point of using the map function is. You can do it with just HTML code, but that requires that you do it over and over.

Avoiding Common Pitfalls

It's the most important thing to remember when rendering lists in React!

4.4 Filtering and Sorting Data – Ordering and Selecting Information

You now know how to create and use arrays, and how to change them to build the right tools. So, you are creating an online store. You want to make it easy to use and to actually find and buy what is out there! The goal of this section is to make it easier to show what you want and to make it all that much more easy to use! To do that, you need to know how to take the data that Javascript offers and to implement all the features that you need!

What will be covered?

*Filtering: How to show only what you want.
*Sorting: How to organize things for the user.

Let's get to it.

Filtering Data: Showing Only What You Need

Filtering involves creating a new array containing only the elements from the original array that meet a specified condition. This is useful for displaying a subset of your data based on user input or other criteria. Javascript provides a number of built-in methods for filtering arrays:

To make sure that you make it well, test the following:

- Use a meaningful function name that clearly describes the filtering criteria (e.g., filterByPrice, filterByCategory).
- Handle edge cases and potential errors gracefully.
- Test your filtering function with a variety of inputs to ensure that it's working correctly.

What are Javascript commands for filtering?

```
const products = [
  { name: 'Laptop', category: 'Electronics', price: 1200 },
  { name: 'Keyboard', category: 'Electronics', price: 75 },
  { name: 'T-Shirt', category: 'Clothing', price: 25 },
  { name: 'Jeans', category: 'Clothing', price: 80 },
];
```

```
const electronics = products.filter(product => product.category ===
'Electronics');
console.log(electronics);
```

A Personal Insight: Here are some things to keep in mind! To help and to get all of those Javascript skills to work and to get all the different commands!

Sorting Data: Putting Elements in Order

Sorting involves rearranging the elements in an array based on a specified criteria. This is useful for displaying data in a logical order, such as by price, name, or date. Javascript provides a number of built-in methods for sorting arrays:

```
    const products = [
  { name: 'Laptop', price: 1200 },
  { name: 'Keyboard', price: 75 },
  { name: 'T-Shirt', price: 25 },
  { name: 'Jeans', price: 80 },
];

products.sort((a, b) => a.price - b.price); // Sort by price (ascending)
console.log(products);
```

However, this mutates (changes) the original array! If you don't want this, try this:

```
    const products = [
  { name: 'Laptop', price: 1200 },
  { name: 'Keyboard', price: 75 },
  { name: 'T-Shirt', category: 'Clothing', price: 25 },
  { name: 'Jeans', category: 'Clothing', price: 80 },
];

const sortedProducts = [...products].sort((a, b) => a.price - b.price);
console.log(sortedProducts)
```

With that, you are now going to want to keep the following in mind:

- Use descriptive variable names that clearly indicate the sorting criteria (e.g., sortByPrice, sortByName).
- Handle edge cases and potential errors gracefully.
- Test your sorting function with a variety of inputs to ensure that it's working correctly.

A Personal Insight: What has also been essential for me is to make test data and to have the tests come in so that it can be easier to find out what code I will need to do!

Chapter 5: Hooks: Reusable Logic in Functional Components – Supercharging Your Components

Alright, so you now know how to display all the different types of Javascript code for that React code! What if you want to make code that is more modular and simple to use? You can now do it with hooks!

You can now use the power of functions while also having the power of code that you saw in components to build the best of what you can do in Javascript.

This chapter will take you through the power of what hooks can offer.

*What are Hooks?

useEffect

Custom Hooks

With that, let's dive in!

5.1 What are Hooks? – Tapping into React's Power

You've built and used components. Javascript can make it all work, and you can show the user what you want. But what if there is more you want to do? What if you want to change the component? Before the modern version of Javascript, there wasn't an easy way to make that happen.

Then, it's time to meet hooks! Think of Hooks as a way to "hook into" React state and lifecycle features from functional components. Hooks let you use React without writing classes. They're functions that let you "hook into" React state and lifecycle features from functional components. Hooks don't work inside classes - they let you use React without classes. They were introduced in React 16.8, and have quickly become the preferred way to manage state and side effects in React components.

This section will cover:

What are hooks? Why are they important?
The basic rules of hooks.
What common hooks are available?

What are Hooks? Function-Based Features

To take it one step further, Javascript does not naturally have a way to create code that changes what it is and does. That means that you can't track what happened. Well, with hooks, it is easy!

There are some rules that you have to look into.

1. You can only call Hooks from functions in React.
2. You can only call hooks at the top level of the function.

If you don't, then it becomes unpredictable what's going to work and what's not, so I highly recommend that you follow that!

A Personal Insight: It can be difficult to understand why these rules are in place. It's all about making sure that the code can be reliable and predictable!

Why Are Hooks Important?

Hooks are an essential tool for modern React development. They allow you to:

- Write more concise and readable code.
- Reuse stateful logic between components.
- Easily manage side effects (e.g., fetching data, setting up subscriptions).
- Avoid the complexities of class components.

A Personal Insight: For me, hooks were the code that unlocked how to make React come to life! With this, you can actually make the code do all the things that people expect from a Javascript page!

5.2 Using useEffect: Side Effects and Lifecycle Management – Making Your Components React to the World

Alright, you know how to manage the state! But to create an actually useful webapp, you need to have the code do things, such as load, pull, and display information! That's where the "useEffect" commands come into play!

useEffect is used to handle side effects in functional components. Side effects are actions that affect something outside of the component itself, such as:

- Fetching data from an API
- Setting up subscriptions or timers
- Directly manipulating the DOM (though this should be done sparingly)

Here's how we will use it!

1. What is the use effect!
2. How to set it up
3. Things to consider

What's the point

This allows you to say what the code should do, such as

- What to do when the code starts
- What to do to change all the different parts.

Without this, the code would just show up and you would have no idea.

A Personal Insight: To me, this is what makes any Javascript code useful and worth the time and effort to put it into place! I can take it from something, and make it into the design!

How to Code It

Alright, so you need to first import it! Let's assume you have the first part down!

Then:

```
    useEffect(() => {
  // Code to run on every render (or when dependencies change)
}, [dependencies]);
```

That is all that it needs! Javascript will have all of it set up.

To break it down:

*The first argument is a function that contains the code you want to execute as a side effect.
*The second argument is an optional array of dependencies.

If you have more than one item that depends on it, it will be called again!

A Personal Insight: It takes time to fully grok what is required to make it all work, but after a while it does!

What to Think About With useEffect

To make all of this work, here are a few things.

*You are not supposed to directly change and affect the state! To do that, you must use another useState!
*Do you want to make it to where it never runs again? Put in an empty array as the second

argument!

*If you are doing anything outside of Javascript, you must create a "clean-up" action!

5.3 Custom Hooks: Extracting Reusable Logic – Your Own Building Blocks

You now know how to use prebuilt hooks to get the job done! Now, you want to unlock all the different kinds of things that you can do. That is where you, the Javascript coder, can create your own hooks to make the code even more useful.

This is where you can then see what parts are useful and to make it to where you can make it all come together more effectively!

In this section, we'll explore how to create custom Hooks in React, allowing you to extract reusable logic and share it across multiple components.

*What will be discussed

*Why should you create it?

*What are the rules to remember?

*How will you implement it?

What are Custom Hooks?

A custom Hook is a JavaScript function whose name starts with "use" and that may call other Hooks. These are used to help make Javascript code easier to read and more effective!

You can then put it all together to make all the functions that you want!

A Personal Insight: After working with Javascript for a while, you will see code that repeats and repeats! That's where it's time to build a framework that is great and easy to use.

Why Use Custom Hooks?

Custom Hooks allow you to:

- Extract reusable stateful logic: If you find yourself writing the same code in multiple components, you can extract that code into a custom Hook.
- Improve code organization: Custom Hooks help to keep your components concise and focused on their core responsibilities.
- Enhance testability: Custom Hooks can be tested independently, making it easier to ensure that your logic is working correctly.

A Personal Insight: I personally found this to be extremely useful, as it reduces the number of copy and pastes I did!

Rules for Custom Hooks

Custom Hooks are functions so what do they do and what do you have to remember?

1. You have to use the command.
2. Use a Capital letter first
3. It can only be called inside a Javascript component, or another custom Hook.
4. Has to be able to call other Hooks.

If not, it's not really a custom hook!

What Does It Look Like: Building It All Together

Let's create a custom Hook that tracks the window size:

```javascript
import { useState, useEffect } from 'react';

function useWindowSize() {
  const [windowSize, setWindowSize] = useState({
    width: window.innerWidth,
    height: window.innerHeight,
  });

  useEffect(() => {
    function handleResize() {
      setWindowSize({
        width: window.innerWidth,
        height: window.innerHeight,
      });
    }

    window.addEventListener('resize', handleResize);

    handleResize(); // Call it initially

    return () => window.removeEventListener('resize', handleResize); // Cleanup
  }, []); // Empty dependency array means this runs only on mount and unmount

  return windowSize;
}
```

Here is what this does:

1. It declares that the function will track the window size and to save it.
2. It checks on the function and then has the event listener start.
3. The return part takes care of what comes next.

You can then implement it with:

```javascript
import React from 'react';
```

```
import useWindowSize from './useWindowSize';

function MyComponent() {
  const windowSize = useWindowSize();

  return (
    <div>
      <p>Window width: {windowSize.width}</p>
      <p>Window height: {windowSize.height}</p>
    </div>
  );
}

export default MyComponent;
```

With that, you are able to see the size of the window!

A Personal Insight: It may seem complicated, but it is all about what is reusable. If you want to make more of those, you will be able to make a much better code structure.

5.4 Common Hooks: useContext, useReducer – Sharing and Managing State

You've now learned about the individual building blocks, but what happens when you have a lot of different components working together? To do that, you need to make sure that you have the ability to manage the states as they interact! There are a few ways to do so, and that's where the hooks useContext and useReducer can be used to change the states and to make them all come together.

In this section, we'll provide a brief overview of these advanced hooks and how they can simplify state management in complex React applications.

What we will cover
*"useContext"
*"useReducer"

useContext: Accessing Global State – Reaching Across the Component Tree

So, what do you do when your code has a whole bunch of children? Is there any way to make the code change or for all to use the same data? That is where the useContext comes to the rescue!

What is the concept?

1. You create a common area where the data will come from.
2. Then, you "provide" that data so that all children can access.

Think of it as a water pipe. If you want to give all the different places access to water, you have to connect to the main water pipe, and then from there, all can access it.

So here's the code:

```
    // 1. Create the Context
const MyContext = React.createContext(defaultValue);

// 2. Create a Provider (usually at the top level of your app)
function App() {
  const [value, setValue] = useState(defaultValue);

  return (
    <MyContext.Provider value={{ value, setValue }}>
      {/* Your components that need access to the context */}
    </MyContext.Provider>
  );
}

// 3. Consume the Context in a Child Component
function MyComponent() {
  const { value, setValue } = useContext(MyContext);

  return (
    <div>
      <p>Value: {value}</p>
      <button onClick={() => setValue(value + 1)}>Increment</button>
    </div>
  );
}
```

The steps are:

1. Create the context with React.createContext. If you give it a value, that is the default.
2. Create a provider that specifies the original code. It has to be in this specific setup.
3. Then, have your components that you want to use, access the code!

A Personal Insight: With all of these, you will be able to create a system that can connect all the different parts of Javascript code.

useReducer: Managing Complex State Logic – A More Structured Approach

What about if you want to make all the code very complicated? That is where you need to manage the code for all the different functions and to make it all set and ready! That's where you need the tool called useReducer!

- **Reducers:** Functions that specify how the state should be updated based on an action.

```
    const reducer = (state, action) => {
  switch (action.type) {
    case 'INCREMENT':
      return { count: state.count + 1 };
    case 'DECREMENT':
      return { count: state.count - 1 };
    default:
```

```
        return state;
    }
};
```

- **Dispatch:** A function used to trigger state updates by dispatching actions to the reducer.

What's the code?

```
    import React, { useReducer } from 'react';

const initialState = { count: 0 };

function reducer(state, action) {
  switch (action.type) {
    case 'increment':
      return {count: state.count + 1};
    case 'decrement':
      return {count: state.count - 1};
    default:
      throw new Error();
  }
}

function Counter() {
  const [state, dispatch] = useReducer(reducer, initialState);
  return (
    <>
      Count: {state.count}
      <button onClick={() => dispatch({type: 'decrement'})}>-</button>
      <button onClick={() => dispatch({type: 'increment'})}>+</button>
    </>
  );
}
```

A Personal Insight: What's very key is to make sure that there are all the codes in place for all of the different actions.

Chapter 6: Forms: Capturing User Input – Gathering Data from Your Users

You've crafted all this great code and are able to use all these different features of Javascript. But what if you want to allow users to use it too? You're going to need a form!

That is what you need, and that is why it is essential to get it all under control! You will be able to make great and powerful things with all of the information you have all set.

In this chapter, we'll explore how to build forms in React, handle form submissions, access form values, validate form data, and manage form state effectively using hooks.

We will cover:

*How to craft HTML forms.

*How to handle different submissions.

*Accessing all those values that have been created.

*How to validate and make sure it is all good.

*Using hooks to make sure it is all there!

6.1 Building Basic Forms – The Foundation of User Input

One of the most common things to create is a form! You need to have a lot of information from people, so it's about having them share it with you.

In this section, we'll explore the fundamental building blocks of HTML forms and how to create them in React. You'll learn how to use input elements, labels, and buttons to create forms that are both functional and user-friendly.

What does that mean for today?
*HTML Structure
*Form Controls:
*Labels:
*Buttons

Let's start with the basics!

A Personal Insight: Forms are the bread and butter of web application development. They're how you collect data from users, and mastering them is essential for building interactive and engaging experiences.

The Foundation: The <form> Element

First, all the building blocks have to start somewhere! The <form> element defines the form itself and acts as a container for all the form controls. You will need to use this to indicate that it is all related! The core that you have to know are:

*The action of the form! This tells where to send the data.
*Method - What type of action is it? What are you planning to do with it?

```
    <form action="#" method="post">
  {/* Form controls go here */}
</form>
```

A Personal Insight: If you have that action wrong, it can then lead to the data going to the wrong place, or if you forget it entirely, to do nothing!

Form Controls: The <input> Element and Friends

The <input> element creates various types of input fields, such as text fields, password fields, email fields, checkboxes, and radio buttons. You'll use this to create all kinds of different options!

The key code that must be implemented is the type command.

- **type="text"**: A basic text input field for single-line text.
- **type="password"**: A password input field. The characters are masked for security.
- **type="email"**: An input field specifically for email addresses, with built-in validation.
- **type="checkbox"**: A checkbox that allows the user to select one or more options.
- **type="radio"**: Radio buttons that allow the user to select only one option from a group.
- **type="number"**: An input field for numeric values, with built-in validation.

You also have to consider the attributes.

What's an attribute?

Well those are the extra commands that the HTML gives to tell what more to do!

- **id**: A unique identifier for the element, used to access it with JavaScript.
- **name**: The name of the input field, used to identify the data when the form is submitted.

- **value**: Specifies the initial value of the input field. For radio buttons and checkboxes, it's the value that will be submitted if the option is selected.
- **placeholder**: Specifies a hint that describes the expected value of the input field. This text is displayed inside the input field when it is empty.
- **required**: Specifies that the input field is required and must be filled out before the form can be submitted.

All of these make your code useful and help improve what's going on!

A Personal Insight: It can be tempting to skip the placeholder, but doing so will make the user experience that much worse! You want to help them and to guide them!

Labels: Providing Context and Accessibility

The <label> element provides a caption for an input field, improving accessibility and making it easier for users to understand the purpose of the field.

Make sure to make all the labels in the code.

Buttons: Triggering Actions

The <button> element creates a clickable button. You can use the <button> element to submit the form or to trigger other actions.

To make the action occur, you need to specify the type.

1. Submit
2. Reset
3. Button

There are the three types!

A Personal Insight: It is much better to use a button than the image, as it is more accessible.

6.2 Handling Form Submission – Taking Control of the Process

You have the form, and now you need to create a way to capture and use that data! There's a challenge. The default Javascript action is to automatically send it somewhere! We don't want that. Instead, we will want to connect this to our Javascript code.

In this section, we'll explore how to handle form submissions in React, preventing the default browser behavior and processing the form data using JavaScript. To do this, we will need to implement a few things:

*Prevent the Default
*Accessing form values
*Handling multiple inputs

With all of that, let's begin!

A Personal Insight: Before I knew how to do it, there was a lot of frustration because the page would just constantly reload!

Preventing Default Behavior: Stop the Reload!

The default behavior of a form submission is to reload the page and send the form data to the URL specified in the action attribute of the <form> element. In most React applications, we want to prevent this default behavior and handle the form submission using JavaScript.

To prevent the default behavior, you can use the preventDefault() method of the event object. This is an example:

```
    const handleSubmit = (event) => {
  event.preventDefault();
  // Your code to process the form data goes here
};

return (
  <form onSubmit={handleSubmit}>
    {/* Form elements */}
  </form>
);
```

You can see that the most important part of this is the "event.preventDefault();" code, since it stops the default action from occurring.

Accessing Form Values: Getting the Data

Once you have a way to stop the form from submitting, you need a way to get the data. You can connect your data and state! Let's think through some code:

```
    import React, { useState } from 'react';

function MyForm() {
  const [name, setName] = useState('');
  const [email, setEmail] = useState('');

  const handleSubmit = (event) => {
    event.preventDefault();
    console.log('Name:', name);
    console.log('Email:', email);
    // You can then send the data to the server

  };
```

```
  return (
    <form onSubmit={handleSubmit}>
      <label>
        Name:
        <input
          type="text"
          value={name}
          onChange={(e) => setName(e.target.value)}
        />
      </label>
      <label>
        Email:
        <input
          type="email"
          value={email}
          onChange={(e) => setEmail(e.target.value)}
        />
      </label>
      <button type="submit">Submit</button>
    </form>
  );
}
```

The function must then have:

- First it has to get the event!
- Then, set all the state.
- When the submit button is pressed, it will then print the output.

A Personal Insight: A great way to double-check that the code has been set up is to have a function that will print the data to the screen, so that you know that all the different connections have been made.

Handling Multiple Inputs

As you are building the code, there are a few ways that you can make the code more efficient.

The main takeaway is that the more you use the more that you can create! So it is up to you to use it! Here is how to do it

```
const [formData, setFormData] = useState({
  name: '',
  email: '',
  message: ''
});

const handleChange = (event) => {
  const { name, value } = event.target;
  setFormData({
    ...formData,
    [name]: value
```

```
    });
};

// ... (In your form) ...
<input type="text" name="name" value={formData.name} onChange={handleChange}
/>
<textarea name="message" value={formData.message} onChange={handleChange} />
```

You have unlocked great power! Use it carefully! With this, you can now make something great!

Anything else that I can help you with?
Where should we go next?

6.3 Accessing Form Values – Retrieving What the User Entered

You now know how to use the elements, and you can add the right Javascript to make it all work. Now, you just have to get the data!

In this section, we'll explore how to access the values that the user has entered into the form fields. This is the key to unlocking the information.

You'll need to:

- Prevent the default form submission behavior.
- Access the form values using JavaScript.
- Display or process the form data.

Preventing Default Behavior: Stop the Reload!

It's not a good experience if every time the user clicks something there is a reload! So you need to make sure that is prevented. To do that, you'll need to use the event.preventDefault().

Here's what it looks like:

```
    const handleSubmit = (event) => {
  event.preventDefault(); // Prevent the default form submission
  // Access and process form values here
};
```

This is what you need and it will be helpful in all future code.

Accessing Form Values: The event.target Property

The most common way to access form values is to use the event.target property. This property refers to the HTML element that triggered the event (in this case, the input field). You can then access the value of the input field using the value property.

To take a look at what it means, let's put it all together!

```
        import React, { useState } from 'react';

function MyForm() {
  const [name, setName] = useState('');
  const [email, setEmail] = useState('');

  const handleSubmit = (event) => {
    event.preventDefault();
    console.log('Name:', name);
    console.log('Email:', email);
    // You can then send the data to the server

  };

  return (
    <form onSubmit={handleSubmit}>
      <label>
        Name:
        <input
          type="text"
          value={name}
          onChange={(e) => setName(e.target.value)}
        />
      </label>
      <label>
        Email:
        <input
          type="email"
          value={email}
          onChange={(e) => setEmail(e.target.value)}
        />
      </label>
      <button type="submit">Submit</button>
    </form>
  );
}
```

To break it down:

1. You create a function called handleSubmit to capture and handle.
2. You prevent it from submitting by calling that function first.
3. After that, you have to then put it all together and create the code to use it! To have a command, you must have the value for the name and use the onChange to call and set the value.

A Personal Insight: This sounds hard to do! One of the most common mistakes I have seen is that either you forget the prevent default or you don't use the right name! So, be careful!

Handling Multiple Inputs: A More Efficient Approach

If you have multiple input fields in your form, it can be tedious to create separate state variables and event handlers for each field. A more efficient approach is to use a single state variable to store all the form data as an object.

To do this, you would use the following Javascript code.

```
    const [formData, setFormData] = useState({
  name: '',
  email: '',
  message: ''
});

const handleChange = (event) => {
  const { name, value } = event.target;
  setFormData({
    ...formData,
    [name]: value
  });
};
```

A Personal Insight: I find that this is what I do for my code more and more! It's extremely helpful to make sure that everything works!

6.4 Validating Form Data – Ensuring Data Quality: Keeping Your App Clean and Secure

Alright! You have a form! And you have the Javascript code that can read from it! You are all set to fly! But, what if the users are putting in the wrong information? Think about how a lot of people need to put in very specific things, such as phone numbers, emails, and passwords. It's those reasons why you need validation!

In this section, we'll explore how to use JavaScript to validate form data on the client-side, ensuring that the data submitted by the user is correct and in the expected format.
What are we going to be coding?

*The types of validation!
*A test to make sure it all works!
*And that you can make it look good!

A Personal Insight: It's all about knowing what you expect! What are your requirements? And to make sure that your code can handle what you expect! You may even want to write it down!

So, What Can You Validate? The Core Checks

1. "Is It There?" Presence Checks

2. "Is It Right?" Format Checks
3. "Is it Correct?" Custom Validations

To run through these, let's think of the following:

*First name
*Email
*Password

Okay so we have that setup. Let's now see what to do with the code!

1. Is It There? Presence Checks

You can't submit a form if you didn't fill all the codes! But what can you do to get there? Well, Javascript has the required command!

```
<input type="text" id="firstName" name="firstName" required />
```

To add to that, you can always add a function that checks to see if the code is not there!

A Personal Insight: In this step, I always make the form as useful and as helpful as I can to make sure that the data the user is seeing is as clear as possible.

2. Is it Right? Format Checks

To see if it's right, you can use all sorts of different code. But again, Javascript helps you!

```
<input type="email" id="email" name="email" required />
```

You can use this and it will tell you if it is not in an e-mail format. There are also a lot of other cases to consider. Such as:

*Phone numbers
*Credit Card numbers

The more you can know what you are testing, the better you can test and make.

3. Is it Correct? Custom Validations

However, sometimes you need something that is a little more specific than the Javascript has to offer. So what you need is the ability to make custom functions and to be able to test.

This can be done with this command

```
function validatePassword(password) {
// Check for minimum length, special characters, etc.
```

```
  if (password.length < 8) {
    return "Password must be at least 8 characters long.";
  }
  // ... More validation rules ...
  return null; // No error message if password is valid
}
```

A Personal Insight: When I was first coding, I didn't know what to test, so nothing ever came up. However, the key is to think about all the different ways people can attack or just make mistakes!

But does it look good?

You need to also think about what the user sees, which is why you need to make sure that you have:

- Clear and concise error messages.
- Inline validation (showing errors as the user types).
- Clear visual cues for invalid fields (e.g., red borders, tooltips).

What you need to also keep in mind is that you are making something for the user! They are the ones that need to see it!

6.5 Managing Form State with Hooks – Keeping Track of Changes

You've created all of these amazing data and you know how to validate! However, how to keep track? What is the best way to take all of that data and to organize it? You want to be able to take all of it and to ensure the best possible things come from it! That's what Hooks do.

In this section, we'll explore the best practices for managing form state with Hooks, including:

- Using useState for individual input fields.
- Using a single state object for multiple inputs.
- Handling different input types (text, numbers, checkboxes, etc.).
- Implementing controlled components.

You'll now have the ability to implement all the different parts into a single structure.

Why Use Hooks for Form State? The Modern Approach

Before Hooks, class components were the primary way to manage state in React. However, Hooks provide a more concise, readable, and reusable way to manage state in functional components. They also eliminate the need for this binding and other complexities associated with class components.

A Personal Insight: For me, hooks are just so much easier than what was there before. I don't have to worry about the code that I was doing.

What you need now is to think about what you are trying to do, and then figure out how to make that work!

Using useState for Individual Input Fields

So, let's consider how you can use all of this to make all the parts work! Here is some Javascript code to think about

```
import React, { useState } from 'react';

function MyForm() {
  const [firstName, setFirstName] = useState('');
  const [lastName, setLastName] = useState('');

  const handleFirstNameChange = (event) => {
    setFirstName(event.target.value);
  };

  const handleLastNameChange = (event) => {
    setLastName(event.target.value);
  };

  return (
    <form>
      <label>
        First Name:
        <input type="text" value={firstName} onChange={handleFirstNameChange}
/>
      </label>
      <label>
        Last Name:
        <input type="text" value={lastName} onChange={handleLastNameChange}
/>
      </label>
    </form>
  );
}
```

With this, you are able to see and set up all the different pieces that need to happen!

A Personal Insight: It may seem like there is too much code to just get the bare minimum going, but it provides a lot of clarity. This is something that really helps and you can test and make sure everything is going great.

Using a Single State Object for Multiple Inputs: Streamlining Your Code

But now you have to deal with a lot of different hooks! How can you make the code more efficient? You want to minimize code, not maximize it!

This is where you can use the set of code to manage all the different changes.

```jsx
import React, { useState } from 'react';

function MyForm() {
  const [formData, setFormData] = useState({
    firstName: '',
    lastName: ''
  });

  const handleChange = (event) => {
    const { name, value } = event.target;
    setFormData({
      ...formData,
      [name]: value
    });
  };

  return (
    <form>
      <label>
        First Name:
        <input
          type="text"
          name="firstName"
          value={formData.firstName}
          onChange={handleChange}
        />
      </label>
      <label>
        Last Name:
        <input
          type="text"
          name="lastName"
          value={formData.lastName}
          onChange={handleChange}
        />
      </label>
    </form>
  );
}
```

To describe this, what you need to know is that the goal is to have something with the code and then make it to where all can see and touch.

A Personal Insight: It's really easy to get lost in the different functions, so I like to take the code and put it somewhere, and to have it running and available.

Chapter 7: Routing: Navigating Between Pages (React Router) – Building a Multi-Page Experience

You now know how to create a Javascript code and implement the different methods that make it all work. What now comes to play is how can you have that Javascript code to create different areas? The main technique is to create routes to manage the different sections of a webpage.

In this chapter, we'll explore React Router, a powerful library that makes it easy to create single-page applications (SPAs) with multiple views. Think of it as building a navigation system for your web app, allowing users to seamlessly move between different sections of your content.

To do that, we need a bunch of things

- What is React Router?

- What are those links for navigation?

- What is dynamic routing?

Let's dive in!

7.1 Introduction to React Router – A Map for Your App: Guiding Users Through Your Website

You can make code that does things and can have all the buttons and switches to do! That's great. What if you have a website that has more than one page? What if it needs to be easy to access, and to show what is there?

That is where the React Router comes in! You can use it to set each page so that it is:
easy to access,
easy to maintain, and
scalable for whatever the future requires!

In this section, we'll set the stage for what we need to do and make it all useful! We'll cover the core concepts of client-side routing and why it's essential for building single-page applications (SPAs).

What is a Router?
*What Can You Do With the Router?
*A Better Way to Navigate

Let's get started!

What is a Router? Directing Traffic Client-Side

To start, Javascript is great! But how do we make it function? That's where it comes in and the way the old HTML pages were.

- "Old": Every time you click, you have to wait for the code to load, and it can be very annoying.
- "New": the code is all set up in advance, and then you just have to see all that it comes.

It also allows you to code and to divide the responsibilities.

A Personal Insight: What's great is that you can separate the components! So, you can focus on the display and someone else can focus on how the code is.

What Can You Do With the Router?

There are lots of different things that the Router allows you to do!

- Dynamic Page Updates:
- Organized Codebase
- Improved User Experience

7.2 Setting Up React Router – Getting Ready to Navigate

You now know what a router is and what it is supposed to do! But to get there, there are some steps that you have to follow in order to actually implement the code to make it all work!

Setting up React Router involves installing the necessary packages and configuring your application to use the router.

What steps do you need to take to get there?

*Install React Router
*The Code to set up BrowserRouter
*Where to place all these new Javascript codes.

A Personal Insight: It is easy to get lost here, so it is helpful to just get the code working, and then you can look at the details!

Installing React Router

Use NPM to install.

```
npm install react-router-dom
```

And as a reminder, that puts it in the dependency section. In this case, react-router-dom is the command to let the browser and the system actually see that's all.

Setting up BrowserRouter

This is where the fun begins!

To do this, you need to have the following code:

```
import { BrowserRouter } from "react-router-dom";

function App() {
  return (
    <BrowserRouter>
      {/* Your application content goes here */}
    </BrowserRouter>
  );
}
```

What's going on?

*BrowserRouter means that it's the kind of router you want to use.
*Then, the rest of your code is what it needs to be.

This makes sure that there is some kind of structure that can be used. However, this doesn't do anything at all! You need to actually define those routes!

A Personal Insight: It is very easy to forget to include the import statement. It is what Javascript uses to help make the code all that easier to do! You aren't coding from a blank page, so make sure to make that so!

7.3 Defining Routes and Components – Connecting URLs to Content: Mapping Your Web App

So, you got all the framework for Reacts set up and you've got the browser running. What's next? You need a path! You have to build the map to where you are going in Javascript. This is all about making it that much easier to implement the code to bring it to life.

Now it's all about how to take that data and to present it as a function.

What needs to be done?
You need to

*Create the different routes.
*Map the components to those routes, and
*Test it!

Let's dive into these steps.

Laying Down the Routes: The <Route> Component

To do all this, you use this one element, which is <Route>. This is a component in React that connects a URL to an element.

All you have to do is specify the path, and you specify what element to show!

```
<Route path="/about" element={<About />} />
<Route path="/contact" element={<Contact />} />
```

A Personal Insight: It is very easy to get into the habit of just coding. But take the time to think of what code you will be using, and that will make it easy to do!

What if you want the Home Page?

Well, the home page has the route /! For example

```
<Route path="/" element={<Home />} />
```

What about 404 pages where nothing is found?

For this, I would recommend using the command "*". It serves as a way to say that if nothing has been found, then to do this!

The code to put all of this together is:

```
import { BrowserRouter, Routes, Route } from "react-router-dom";
import Home from "./pages/Home";
import About from "./pages/About";
import Contact from "./pages/Contact";
import NotFound from "./pages/NotFound";

function App() {
  return (
    <BrowserRouter>
      <Routes>
        <Route path="/" element={<Home />} />
        <Route path="/about" element={<About />} />
        <Route path="/contact" element={<Contact />} />
        <Route path="*" element={<NotFound />} />
```

```
    </Routes>
  </BrowserRouter>
);
}
```

To break this down:

1. First, you are connecting the code.
2. Then you are making the parts to do the code!
3. If it does not work, it goes to not found.

A Personal Insight: There is one small part that may be confusing, and it is the use of element. This is just how they chose to call the component that will be displayed.

7.4 Using <Link> and <NavLink> for Navigation – Guiding Your Users

You've set up your routes, but how do you let users actually *navigate* between them? You need a way to create links that don't cause a full page reload, providing a smooth and responsive user experience. That's where <Link> and <NavLink> come in!

Think of these components as your navigation tools, allowing users to effortlessly move between different sections of your web application.

This section will cover:

- The use of <Link> to create navigational links.
- The use of <NavLink> to indicate the active route.

<Link>: The Basic Navigation Tool

The <Link> component from react-router-dom is used to create links that perform client-side navigation. This means that when a user clicks on a <Link>, React Router will update the URL and render the corresponding component without reloading the entire page.

Let's set up the code:

```
import { Link } from "react-router-dom";

function Navigation() {
  return (
    <nav>
      <ul>
        <li>
          <Link to="/">Home</Link>
        </li>
        <li>
          <Link to="/about">About</Link>
        </li>
        <li>
```

```
          <Link to="/contact">Contact</Link>
        </li>
      </ul>
    </nav>
  );
}
```

To break it down:

You need to first use import to let the Javascript know what you are working on.
Then, you have to use the to command to set where it goes.

A Personal Insight: It is tempting to just use HTML, but that defeats the entire purpose of having a single page website, and you would have to reload.

<NavLink>: Highlighting the Active Route

The <NavLink> component is similar to the <Link> component, but it also provides a way to style the active route (the route that is currently being displayed). This can be useful for highlighting the current page in a navigation menu.

What's the code to use?

```
import { NavLink } from "react-router-dom";

function Navigation() {
  return (
    <nav>
      <ul>
        <li>
          <NavLink
            to="/"
            className={({ isActive }) => (isActive ? 'active' : 'inactive')}
          >
            Home
          </NavLink>
        </li>
        <li>
          <NavLink
            to="/about"
            className={({ isActive }) => (isActive ? 'active' : 'inactive')}
          >
            About
          </NavLink>
        </li>
      </ul>
    </nav>
  );
}
```

What's key to remember is the className! As it knows what to do.

A Personal Insight: I really like this feature. It is a great way to show what is going on in the website and to show what the user is expecting to do.

7.5 Route Parameters: Passing Data in the URL – Making Dynamic Links

You now know how to connect the buttons to different websites. However, what if you want the URL to change dynamically? What if you want to pass a specific number, name, or anything else to the next URL?

That's the goal of route parameters!

In this section, we'll explore how to use route parameters to create dynamic URLs that can pass data to your React components. This allows you to create more flexible and data-driven applications.
*Then we will discuss the code and the best ways to use it.
*I'll also give you the different tips to make sure you understand it.

With that, let's begin!

What are Route Parameters?

Route parameters are dynamic segments of a URL that can be used to pass data to a React component. They are defined using a colon : followed by the parameter name.

For example, in the route /users/:id, :id is a route parameter that represents the ID of a user.

What are the different things that you need to think about?

1. How do you define the route?
2. How do you access them?

Defining Routes with Parameters: Setting the Stage

To define a route with parameters, you use the <Route> component from react-router-dom, just like you did in the previous section. However, you'll also need to include the parameter name in the path prop, prefixed with a colon :.

```
<Route path="/products/:productId" element={<ProductDetail />} />
```

In this example, the /products/:productId route defines a parameter called productId. This means that any URL that matches this pattern (e.g., /products/123, /products/abc) will be routed to the ProductDetail component.

A Personal Insight: As you can see, there are a lot of different things you can use and set up. But that is the challenge and the fun of using Javascript!

Accessing Route Parameters: Unlocking the Data

To access the value of a route parameter within a component, you can use the useParams() Hook from react-router-dom. This Hook returns an object that contains all the route parameters for the current route.

Here's how to use the useParams() Hook:

```
import { useParams } from 'react-router-dom';

function ProductDetail() {
  const { productId } = useParams();

  return (
    <div>
      <h1>Product Details</h1>
        <p>Product ID: {productId}</p>
    </div>
  );
}
```

This is what you need to actually get the code to work!

A Personal Insight: This is a small thing, but it is easy to forget to import the function, which is why I always make sure to have it at the top of my code!

Chapter 8: Making API Requests: Fetching Data from a Server – Bringing the Outside World In

So you've created a Javascript code that can show different pages. The next important part is to be able to get the information from all the different areas! In the modern world, this means the server! You'll need to master Javascript so you can make use of external APIs.

In this chapter, we'll discuss:

*What's the Javascript Fetch API

*Making basic requests

*How to handle the information,

*How to actually implement it, and,

*What to do to handle errors!

With that, let's begin!

8.1 Understanding the Fetch API – Your Window to the Web: Talking to Servers

You have all this amazing Javascript code. Now, it's time to connect with other parts of the world! You can do that with the Fetch API! To get information from other websites, you have to contact them! Then, you can show all of this off.

The Fetch API provides a modern and powerful way to make network requests in JavaScript. Think of it as your window to the web, allowing you to fetch data from servers, send data to servers, and perform other types of network operations.
The goal of this is to make a connection and then send data.

This section will cover:

- What is the Fetch API?
- Why use the Fetch API?
- How does it actually work?

Let's get to it!

What is the Fetch API? A Modern Approach to Network Requests

The Fetch API provides a clean and intuitive interface for making network requests. It replaces the older XMLHttpRequest object, which was more complex and less flexible.

Here's the basic syntax for using the Fetch API:

```
    fetch(url)
.then(response => {
  // Handle the response
})
.catch(error => {
  // Handle errors
});
```

What is then happening is that Javascript is sending a signal to that URL, and getting information back! It's like calling a friend.

Why Use the Fetch API?

The Fetch API offers several advantages over the older XMLHttpRequest object:

- **Simplicity:** The Fetch API is easier to use and understand than XMLHttpRequest.
- **Promises:** The Fetch API is based on Promises, which makes it easier to handle asynchronous operations.
- **Flexibility:** The Fetch API supports a wide range of request options, allowing you to customize your requests as needed.
- **Modern Standard:** The Fetch API is the modern standard for making network requests in JavaScript and is supported by all major browsers.

What do you do?

1. You have to set up what code to use!
2. Then you have to use the code!

A Personal Insight: At first, I was very confused and didn't quite understand why we had to move on from the XMLHttpRequest object, but after I used it for a while, I really understood how it is a lot more intuitive and easier to use.

How Does It Actually Work? A Step-by-Step Breakdown

1. **fetch(url):** This initiates a network request to the specified URL. It returns a Promise that resolves to the *Response* to that request, whether it is successful or not.
2. **.then(response => { ... }):** This handles the response from the server. The response object contains information about the response, such as the status code, headers, and body.
   - response.ok: A boolean property that indicates whether the response was successful (status code in the 200-299 range).

- response.json(): A method that parses the response body as JSON. This method also returns a Promise.
- response.text(): A method that reads the response body as plain text. This method also returns a Promise.
- response.blob(): A method that reads the response body as a Blob (Binary Large Object). This is useful for handling images and other binary data.

3. **.then(data => { ... }):** This handles the parsed data. If the response is successful and the response body is parsed successfully, this block will be executed. The data variable will contain the parsed data (e.g., a JSON object, a string, or a Blob).

4. **.catch(error => { ... }):** This handles any errors that occur during the process, such as network errors or parsing errors. The error variable will contain information about the error.

A Personal Insight: Always check the response.ok property to make sure that the request was successful before attempting to parse the response body. This can help you to avoid unexpected errors.

8.2 Making GET Requests – Getting Data from the Server

To do this, you just have to use the function fetch. It is not a Javascript function, but a browser function! If you use it, then it has to be run in the browser!

To use it, it looks like this:

```
fetch('https://api.example.com/data')

  .then(response => response.json())

  .then(data => console.log(data))

  .catch(error => console.error('Error:', error));
```

With that, you can do a lot to make that happen. However, to do it, you need to do those functions every time!

A Personal Insight: I have worked with Javascript a lot and I feel like I am always copying and pasting this code! To solve it, I create a function to handle it!

8.2 Making GET Requests – Getting Data from the Server: Your First Data Fetch

You know what the API is and the basic structure. Now, how do you get it to use the data? Well, this is all about GET requests. Think of GET requests as asking the server for information. "Hey can you give me XYZ?"

In this section, we'll explore how to use the Fetch API to make GET requests, retrieve data from servers, and display it in your React components.

These are the steps:
**What to say to fetch it.
How to make the code display it in your code.
And what's a great test to see if the code works?

Let's dive in!

Getting the Ball Rolling: Making the Fetch Request

To get the code working, you first need to use the fetch() method. This may be a given, but remember that you have to ask for the data before you can do anything,

```
    fetch('https://api.example.com/data')
.then(response => {
  // Process the response
})
.catch(error => {
  // Handle errors
});
```

This is like telling the server "Hey, I'm here, give me what you have!"

Getting the Data: Javascript code

The response to that may be just a message, such as 404 or that a server has encountered a problem. You need to actually get the data, so to do that, add another line of code!

```
    fetch('https://api.example.com/data')
.then(response => response.json()) // Parse the response as JSON
.then(data => {
  // Process the data
})
```

```
  .catch(error => {
    // Handle errors
  });
```

What you can now do is then to read and see what's going on with the data. You may want to also think about

To test that you have it right, you should remember all the different kinds and types that you are testing!

A Personal Insight: I recommend that for you to test it all, that you think about the data that's being returned.

The different Javascript codes

So what can you do with all of this? Let's create a component that can do it all, from the start!

```
    import React, { useState, useEffect } from 'react';

function MyComponent() {
  const [data, setData] = useState(null);
  const [loading, setLoading] = useState(true);
  const [error, setError] = useState(null);

  useEffect(() => {
    fetch('https://api.example.com/data')
      .then(response => {
        if (!response.ok) {
          throw new Error(`HTTP error! status: ${response.status}`);
        }
        return response.json();
      })
      .then(data => {
        setData(data);
        setLoading(false);
      })
      .catch(error => {
        setError(error);
        setLoading(false);
      });
  }, []); // Empty dependency array means this effect runs only once, after
the initial render

  if (loading) {
    return <p>Loading...</p>;
  }

  if (error) {
    return <p>Error: {error.message}</p>;
  }

  return (
    <div>
```

```
        <h1>Data from API:</h1>
        <pre>{JSON.stringify(data, null, 2)}</pre>
     </div>
  );
}

export default MyComponent;
```

Here are the key pieces that you will need.

- useState is what tracks
- useEffect is what you do when things are starting.
- `` - This is a tag that will properly display

All of this will take a lot of code, but with that, it is done! You now have all the different commands that you need and what's key.

A Personal Insight: It may take some time to get used to, but it is a good skill to have and to remember.

8.3 Handling Responses: JSON and Error Handling – Decoding the Server's Reply

You've learned how to make GET requests, but what happens when the server responds? How do you extract the data from the response and handle potential errors? That's what this section is all about!

This is the next step that will be considered to make sure that the system works and is useful. Think about it like this, if you don't do this, then the code is just going to keep running, and the machine has no idea what is going on.

We will be exploring:

*What to do with the JSON object.
*Dealing with Errors.

JSON: The Language of APIs

JSON (JavaScript Object Notation) is a lightweight data-interchange format that is widely used by APIs. It's a human-readable format that is easy to parse and generate in JavaScript.

A JSON object consists of key-value pairs, similar to JavaScript objects. Here's an example:

```
  {
  "userId": 1,
  "id": 1,
  "title": "delectus aut autem",
  "completed": false
```

```
}
```

To actually get the information from that API! Then, what to do?

If the fetch call is successful, the response object will contain the data from the server. However, the data is typically in a format that is not directly usable by JavaScript. Therefore, you need to parse the response body to extract the data.

For JSON data, you can use the response.json() method:

```
    fetch('https://jsonplaceholder.typicode.com/todos/1')
.then(response => response.json()) // Parse the response as JSON
.then(data => {
  console.log(data); // Output the parsed JSON data
})
.catch(error => {
  console.error('Error fetching data:', error);
});
```

A Personal Insight: I often use a JSON viewer to inspect the structure of the JSON data and to identify the properties I need to access.

Handling Errors: What if Things Go Wrong?

There are a lot of things that can go wrong.

What if the link is wrong?
What if the server is down?
What if the file does not exist?

You won't get anything out of it and you can make it so that there are different things that can be done with it!

That's why you need to handle the errors!

For this, you need to add a catch command to the fetch.

```
    fetch('https://jsonplaceholder.typicode.com/todos/1')
.then(response => {
  if (!response.ok) {
    throw new Error(`HTTP error! status: ${response.status}`);
  }
  return response.json();
})
.then(data => {
  console.log(data);
})
.catch(error => {
  console.error('Error fetching data:', error);
```

```
});
```

These are what this code does:

1. The response is what was gotten from the original fetch.
2. If the response.ok is not correct, then it throws a new error!
3. All of this code is then listed as code that will be used.

A Personal Insight: It's easy to get caught up in the happy path and forget about error handling. But robust error handling is essential for building reliable applications that can gracefully handle unexpected situations.

8.4 Using useEffect to Fetch Data – Bringing Data into Your Components

You now know how to use Javascript to get the data. The next challenge is to get it into your React component! That's what we will be tackling!

Here are the main things to do:

- The Basics of useEffect
- How to fetch the Data
- What is the point?

Let's start!

The Basics of useEffect

You've heard me mention this command a few times, but if you want to use a React component, there is nothing more important than to use the useEffect command! It is what can make the program run and to make it all great!

You can use this code:

```
useEffect(() => {
// Side effect code (e.g., fetching data)
return () => {
  // Cleanup code (optional)
};
}, [dependencies]);
```

To break down the code:

- The first argument is a function that contains the code you want to execute as a side effect.
- The second argument is an optional array of dependencies.

If that last part is empty, then you should only call it once!

A Personal Insight: As a general rule, you can always just call the code without anything in the array, but that can lead to a lot of unnecessary processing!

Putting it all together

Okay, so how do you now actually use this to fetch the data? Let's create a component that makes the calls and then uses it!

```jsx
import React, { useState, useEffect } from 'react';

function MyComponent() {
  const [data, setData] = useState(null);
  const [loading, setLoading] = useState(true);
  const [error, setError] = useState(null);

  useEffect(() => {
    fetch('https://api.example.com/data')
      .then(response => {
        if (!response.ok) {
          throw new Error(`HTTP error! status: ${response.status}`);
        }
        return response.json();
      })
      .then(data => {
        setData(data);
        setLoading(false);
      })
      .catch(error => {
        setError(error);
        setLoading(false);
      });
  }, []); // Empty dependency array means this effect runs only once, after
the initial render

  if (loading) {
    return <p>Loading...</p>;
  }

  if (error) {
    return <p>Error: {error.message}</p>;
  }

  return (
    <div>
      <h1>Data from API:</h1>
      <pre>{JSON.stringify(data, null, 2)}</pre>
    </div>
  );
}

export default MyComponent;
```

And that is all it takes! To make this code work you will also need to

1. Create a lot of different types of useStates.
2. You will have to remember to create a function that checks for success!
3. Test and make sure it all works!

A Personal Insight: There is a lot of boilerplate code that I tend to copy and paste, so it helps to have a template that you can use!

8.5 Loading States and Error Handling – Keeping Your Users Informed and Happy

You now have the ability to fetch data and to transfer all that data! There are always some problems, such as the system taking too long to load. In that case, you want to be able to tell your users!

In this section, we'll explore how to use loading states and error handling to provide a smooth and informative user experience when fetching data from a server.

Now, what needs to be considered?
*There are different states that need to be considered!
*What's the best way to handle it?

Alright, let's take a look!

The Importance of Managing the User Experience

The goal is to think about what the user wants, and what they need to know!

What is the user seeing? There are three possible screens:

- Loading: Please wait!
- Data: The data!
- Error: Something bad happened.

Remember our goal: We don't want the user to see a frozen or broken Javascript page.

Implementing Loading States: Letting the User Know You're Working

When fetching data from a server, it can take some time for the data to arrive. During this time, it's important to provide feedback to the user to let them know that the application is working and that their request is being processed.

This can be done with the state and the use effect!

```
    const [isLoading, setIsLoading] = useState(true); // Start with loading
set to true
```

That is then called during the useEffect!

Then, after getting the data, you have to remember to set it to false!

```
.then(() => {
  setIsLoading(false);
})
```

With that, you have to now create a code for the HTML!

```
{isLoading && <p>Loading data...</p>}
```

This way, it will only display it during a loading time!

A Personal Insight: If you want to make it look fancy, there are also CSS frameworks that can make a loading wheel or other animations!

Handling Errors: Providing Graceful Recovery

It's also important to handle errors gracefully! For that, it is important to show something!

To do that, you would have to set up an error state.

```
const [error, setError] = useState(null);
```

Then, you have to set that variable to whatever error that you want. And then that will become a problem for the users!

I would also recommend that you always show what the error is so you can debug.

A Personal Insight: Here is a reminder! If you use a third party, you have to also consider that you are also depending on them!

Chapter 9: Styling React Applications – Making Your UI Shine

You've learned how to build dynamic and interactive React components, and how to fetch data from servers. You now need to make it be useful and engaging.

In this chapter, we'll explore the different ways to style React applications, from basic inline styles to more advanced techniques like CSS Modules and Styled Components.

We will be covering:

- Inline Styles: Simple, But Limited

- CSS Classes and External Style Sheets: The Classic Approach

- CSS Modules: Scoped Styling

- Styled Components: CSS-in-JS

With that, you'll have all the skills you need to make visually appealing and maintainable React applications. Let's get started!

9.1 Inline Styles – Quick and Dirty Styling: The Simplest Approach

Alright, you have all that Javascript code, and now you need to make it look good. What if you just want a quick and dirty way to style something? That is where inline styles come to play!

Inline styles are the most basic way to style React components. They involve directly adding style attributes to HTML elements within your JSX code. It's quick and easy for simple styling, but not recommended for larger projects.

What are the pluses and minuses?
*How does it actually get done?

That is all that you need to know to create and make something new! The key is to always be testing, so that you can always make sure it functions.

How Do You Make It?

You must first remember! This is not HTML! It is Javascript, so there are some different ways to think about it.

14. It takes in an object, not a string.
24. The CSS properties are camelCased.

That's really it! Here is what it looks like:

```
    <p style={{ color: 'red', backgroundColor: 'lightgray' }}>
  This is a paragraph with inline styles.
</p>
```

What if you want to use this multiple times? Well, you can store it in a variable!

```
    const paragraphStyle = {
  color: 'red',
  backgroundColor: 'lightgray',
  padding: '10px',
};

<p style={paragraphStyle}>
  This is a paragraph with inline styles.
</p>
```

A Personal Insight: For me, this is the best way to quickly test what styles I want for the elements, and then I can take that and put it into a CSS file for better code.

What are the Benefits?

- Easy to implement and what you will likely see when starting out.
- All the code is in Javascript.

That said, there are a lot of problems that you have to consider:

- Code Redundancy
- Maintenance Nightmare
- Limited Styling Options
- Specificity Issues

That is why it is generally not recommended to do.

A Personal Insight: One of the best things to do, as you now know the basics, is to set up a CSS file and use that to make all the code that much easier to test and to run!

9.2 CSS Classes and External Style Sheets – The Traditional Approach: Building a Strong Foundation

You now know how to style code with Javascript in-line, so you are all set. However, it can be a bit messy if you want to reuse styles, so that Javascript code can look weird and have problems.

This is where you should start thinking about CSS and external style sheets.

So, what does it all mean

*You have to learn and use CSS
*Keep the code separate
*Have the best of both worlds with Javascript and with CSS!

That is what we shall review!

A Personal Insight: This is the part where the code starts to look more real and more professional! It takes time to learn CSS, but it's well worth the time.

CSS: What does it mean to Javascript

There are a few basics that you should always keep in mind:

- "class" is now className
- The names are camelCase.
- The structure is in a separate file.

With that, you can then create a connection to the Javascript code with this:

```
const MyComponent = () => {
return (
  <div className="my-component">
    <h1>Hello, world!</h1>
  </div>
);
};
```

The key is the className as that is what the Javascript actually reads! The other thing that Javascript does is to put it into camelCase so that it is different from other HTML codes.

What Does it Look Like For CSS?

Well, you don't have to change a thing! Just do what you want!

```
.my-component {
background-color: lightblue;
padding: 10px;
}
```

A Personal Insight: I always make sure that I put a lot of comments in the code so that people can see what is going on, and all that it means!

9.3 CSS Modules: Scoped Styling – Localizing Your Styles: Avoiding Global CSS Chaos

You now know the basics of CSS and how to use that in Javascript code. But what if you have lots of different components to work with?

That's where CSS Modules come in! These are great because:
*They are local to the files
*It can prevent the wrong things from being styled

This will be a big step in the right direction. You'll want to start by

*Installing the code!
*Importing the code!
*And then using it!

Installing CSS Modules

Most of the time it is already setup. But if not, here is what you should do!

You will need to first do this with your Javascript.

1. Create a file called webpack.config.js
2. Add the code to that file!

```
module.exports = {
  module: {
    rules: [
      {
        test: /\.module\.css$/,
        use: [
          'style-loader',
          {
            loader: 'css-loader',
            options: {
              modules: true,
              localIdentName: '[name]__[local]--[hash:base64:5]',
            },
          },
        ],
      },
    ],
  },
};
```

Make sure that it is there!

A Personal Insight: There are a lot of things that can go wrong with this, and it's hard to debug! Make sure you look up the official documentation to make sure that you are using the right version!

Importing CSS Modules

With that, you have to import the code!

Just do

```
import styles from './MyComponent.module.css';
```

Note the file name, it must end with .module.css!

Using CSS Modules

Now, you can use the styles from the CSS Module.

```
import styles from './MyComponent.module.css';
function MyComponent() {
  return (
    <div className={styles.container}>
      <h1 className={styles.title}>Hello, world!</h1>
    </div>
  );
}
```

And that is it!

A Personal Insight: I like to take a moment and just read over what all the commands mean!

9.4 Styled Components: CSS-in-JS (Brief Overview) – The New Way to Style

You now have seen the different ways to style a Javascript file, now it's time to talk about a new thing that helps keep all of those together and all that you need.

Styled components are designed to help Javascript stay modular and to reduce the amount of files to manage.

But what are the benefits?
*Why is it worth using?
*How to best implement it?

In this section, we'll provide a brief overview of styled components, a popular CSS-in-JS library that allows you to write CSS directly within your JavaScript components. This approach offers several advantages, such as improved code organization, reduced CSS specificity conflicts, and dynamic styling capabilities.

What are Styled Components?

Styled components are a CSS-in-JS library that allows you to write CSS code directly within your Javascript, making it that much easier to transfer it. At its core, it's just about making a JS function!

```
    const StyledButton = styled.button`
background-color: #4CAF50; /* Green */
border: none;
color: white;
padding: 15px 32px;
text-align: center;
text-decoration: none;
display: inline-block;
font-size: 16px;
margin: 4px 2px;
cursor: pointer;
`;
```

What is also great is that it can inherit other properties from the function so that you can have more Javascript in the CSS!

Why Use Styled Components?

- Component-Level Styles:
- Dynamic Styling:
- Improved Readability:

The key is that everything is connected, and you can just do it all.

A Personal Insight: What I have found is that it is just a different way to code and to get everything to work. I recommend that as long as the team is aligned and can see the benefit, it's a useful way to code.

How to use Styled Components

1. Install styled components

```
npm install styled-components
```

Then, you can call all the different parts as you want to see them!

Chapter 10: Putting It All Together: Mini-Projects – Your React Portfolio Starts Here!

Alright, you've absorbed a ton of information, and now it's time to unleash your creativity and build something real. This chapter is all about putting your React skills to the test with a series of engaging mini-projects.

It isn't about memorizing what is said, it is about you actually experimenting. If you don't then you won't be able to get all the Javascript running!

This chapter will focus on the structure to follow so that you can make it yourself:

- o All the different building blocks to do it.

- o All of the different things that you should be doing.

- o And to be able to test and repeat it.

Let's start by going through what will be implemented and what skills you'll need!

A Personal Insight: I'm not going to lie, when I first started coding, it was just me copying and pasting. It wasn't until I made my own project and struggled that I really understood the key points to what was going on and how to use it all!

10.1 Project 1: Simple Todo App – Mastering State and Lists: Putting Your Skills to Work

You've learned about components, JSX, state, events, styling, and all the different parts of Javascript. Now, it's time to put it all together and to build an application! You will find that the challenge of a project is often very different from what you are thinking of, so it's great to just dive in and try it!

This section will guide you through the process of building a simple to-do list application using React, providing a practical and hands-on learning experience.

What should it do? It should have the ability to:
*Add new tasks to a list
*Mark tasks as complete
*Delete tasks from the list

That's it! If you can do that, you have the basics down!

Project Planning: Breaking It Down

Before you start coding, it's helpful to break down the project into smaller, more manageable tasks.

- o Set up the basic code.
- o Create the List component to display the list of to-do items.
- o Add the ability to add new items to the list.
- o Add the ability to check off an item that is done.
- o Add the ability to delete items from the list.
- o Style!

o Set up the basic code:

```jsx
import React, { useState } from 'react';
import './App.css';

function App() {
  return (
    <div className="App">
      <h1>My To-Do List</h1>
      {/* Add components here */}
    </div>
  );
}

export default App;
```

This should be what you do every time!
A Personal Insight: If the very first line doesn't work, then nothing else will. Always start with that!

o Creating the List Component

To display the content, you must then make sure that it is something that you can see.

```jsx
function TodoList({ todos, onToggle, onDelete }) {
  return (
    <ul>
      {todos.map(todo => (
        <li key={todo.id}>
          <span style={{ textDecoration: todo.completed ? 'line-through' :
'none' }}
                onClick={() => onToggle(todo.id)}>
            {todo.text}
          </span>
          <button onClick={() => onDelete(todo.id)}>Delete</button>
        </li>
      ))}
    </ul>
  );
```

```
}
```

And this is where the magic comes to life! The span will say what has to be done in a bit, but this is what you need to start.

- o **Add the Code to Add New Items**

To add new items, you have to first be able to get the code!

```
const [newTodo, setNewTodo] = useState('');
```

Then, you have to make sure that there is a way to save the code.

```
const addTodo = () => {
  if (newTodo.trim() !== '') {
    setTodos([...todos, { id: Date.now(), text: newTodo, completed: false
}]);
    setNewTodo('');
  }
};
```

All you need to do is then use the spread operator, and you are set!

A Personal Insight: It is very easy to forget the spread operator!

- o **Check off the item**

This Javascript code changes what is selected and what is not!

```
const toggleTodo = (id) => {
  setTodos(todos.map(todo =>
    todo.id === id ? { ...todo, completed: !todo.completed } : todo
  ));
};
```

- o **Delete Items from the List**

Finally, you need to be able to clear off all the things from the list!

```
const deleteTodo = (id) => {
  setTodos(todos.filter(todo => todo.id !== id));
};
```

And to put it all together!

You now have the code to test and make all the different things to have and you are set to create a Javascript project that can be very helpful to you and to all those others who want to make something great!

A Personal Insight: One of the most challenging things to do is to actually run through and do the test and to make sure that it all works!

10.2 Project 2: Basic Blog with Posts – Routing and Data Display: Sharing Your Thoughts with the World

You've created a to do list, and now you can track the data! The next challenge for you is to then create a website with multiple pages. That's where you create a blog!

In this section, we'll explore how to use React Router to create a multi-page blog application with a home page, a list of posts, and individual post pages. You'll also learn how to fetch data from a dummy API and display it in your components.

This section will involve:

*Setting up React Router
*Creating a component to show the posts.
*A way to show individual posts.

Let's begin!

Setting Up React Router: Getting Ready to Navigate

We have already spoken about this, but it involves the code:

```
npm install react-router-dom
```

Now you just need to set it up! To make it all come together, just remember to use the same steps to test if it works.

A Personal Insight: I found that it's always a good idea to double-check what you have and to see if the code is there! It's very easy to skip.

Creating a Component to Display Posts: The PostList

The next step is to create a Javascript code that you can use to show off the posts!

```
import React from 'react';
import { Link } from 'react-router-dom';

function PostList({ posts }) {
  return (
    <ul>
      {posts.map(post => (
        <li key={post.id}>
          <Link to={`/posts/${post.id}`}>{post.title}</Link>
```

```
      </li>
    ))}
  </ul>
);
}

export default PostList;
```

What that code will do is make a list! You can see the name, and a brief description!

Creating a Component to Display Individual Posts: The PostDetail

Finally, you need a place to actually show the detail! Here is the code that will show that:

```
import React from 'react';
import { useParams } from 'react-router-dom';

function PostDetail({ posts }) {
  const { postId } = useParams();
  const post = posts.find(post => post.id === parseInt(postId));

  if (!post) {
    return <div>Post not found</div>;
  }

  return (
    <div>
      <h1>{post.title}</h1>
      <p>{post.content}</p>
    </div>
  );
}

export default PostDetail;
```

Remember that you first need to get the data!

Then, the code is set! You are now able to have different pages with the correct details!

A Personal Insight: It can be tempting to just try and copy this code and expect it all to work. But take a moment and try to understand what is going on! That way you know what you can do for the code.

Where to go?

What is now needed is for you to code and create your version of the Javascript. After all, it's all about what you can do!

10.3 Project 3: Interactive Quiz Application – Event Handling and Logic: Testing Knowledge, Having Fun!

You can make Javascript code that shows different pages and what the user is seeing. Let's put it all together with a quiz! In this section, you will use all of your Javascript knowledge to create something that actually tests and challenges the user.

In this section, we'll explore how to build a simple quiz application using React. You'll learn how to:

- "Structure the Data
- "Handle the different parts of the quiz
- "Make it all work.

A Personal Insight: There is something that can be said that if you make a quiz, it shows that you can control the flow and that you can use all of the different elements that a programmer should be able to use.

Structuring the Quiz Data: Questions and Answers

The first step is to design the structure of your quiz data. You can represent each question as an object with the following properties:

- questionText: The text of the question.
- options: An array of answer options.
- correctAnswer: The index of the correct answer in the options array.

Here's an example:

```
    const quizData = [
  {
    questionText: 'What is the capital of France?',
    options: ['London', 'Paris', 'Berlin', 'Rome'],
    correctAnswer: 1
  },
  {
    questionText: 'What is the highest mountain in the world?',
    options: ['K2', 'Mount Everest', 'Kangchenjunga', 'Lhotse'],
    correctAnswer: 1
  }
];
```

This data has to then be structured such that the Javascript can show it all to the users.

Creating the Quiz Component: Displaying Questions and Handling User Input

Now, with the data in hand, you can actually create the quiz! You will need to use all of the functions from before. A function, called Quiz that contains all the different parts of code.

1. Have a command to set the question number to something.
2. Have it show the questions
3. When an answer is clicked, call the code and see if it is correct.
4. Show the next question or that it is complete.

Here is some code to demonstrate:

```
       import React, { useState } from 'react';

function Quiz() {
  const [currentQuestion, setCurrentQuestion] = useState(0);
  const [score, setScore] = useState(0);
  const [showScore, setShowScore] = useState(false);

  const handleClick = (isCorrect) => {
    if (isCorrect) {
      setScore(score + 1);
    }

    const nextQuestion = currentQuestion + 1;
    if (nextQuestion < quizData.length) {
      setCurrentQuestion(nextQuestion);
    } else {
      setShowScore(true);
    }
  };

  return (
    <div className="app">
      {showScore ? (
        <div className="score-section">You scored {score} out of
{quizData.length}</div>
      ) : (
        <>
          <div className="question-section">
            <div className="question-count">
              <span>Question {currentQuestion + 1}</span>/{quizData.length}
            </div>
            <div className="question-
text">{quizData[currentQuestion].questionText}</div>
          </div>
          <div className="answer-section">
            {quizData[currentQuestion].options.map((answerOption, index) => (
              <button onClick={() => handleClick(index ===
quizData[currentQuestion].correctAnswer)}>{answerOption}</button>
            ))}
          </div>
        </>
      )}
```

```
        </div>
    );
}
```

A Personal Insight: From this, it can be easier to just copy and paste that code to implement it all. Just make sure that you have the appropriate codes and whatnot.

10.4 Project 4: E-commerce Product Listing – Data Fetching and Display: Building a Storefront

You have now created a quiz that tests people and sees what they know! However, the next challenge is to get a more real-world application and for that, it's time to create an e-commerce product listing.
In this project, you'll learn how to:

- Fetch product data from a dummy API.
- Display the product data in a visually appealing list.
- Handle loading states and error conditions.
- Use CSS to style the product listing.

We will be focusing on the actual data, so:

- What is the API that will be looked into?
- How to fetch it?
- Then how to display it?

With that, let's start!

A Personal Insight: There is something really cool about seeing the code and knowing it can be used and changed and to have it all set and ready to go! It's like you are coding the next big thing!

Where to Get the Data

There are many online APIs that you can use. A good test, for now, would be https://fakestoreapi.com/products, which provides some data that you can use to play with!

It will come to you as JSON, so you might as well get used to it!

A Personal Insight: The key for this is to not be afraid of all the different APIs and all the different pieces that are all out there. What is key is to just pick one and to go with it!

Here is the code to download:

```
import React, { useState, useEffect } from 'react';
```

```
function ProductList() {
  const [products, setProducts] = useState([]);
  const [loading, setLoading] = useState(true);
  const [error, setError] = useState(null);

  useEffect(() => {
    fetch('https://fakestoreapi.com/products')
      .then(response => {
        if (!response.ok) {
          throw new Error(`HTTP error! status: ${response.status}`);
        }
        return response.json();
      })
      .then(data => {
        setProducts(data);
        setLoading(false);
      })
      .catch(error => {
        setError(error);
        setLoading(false);
      });
  }, []);

  if (loading) {
    return <p>Loading products...</p>;
  }

  if (error) {
    return <p>Error: {error.message}</p>;
  }

  return (
    <div className="product-list">
      {products.map(product => (
        <div key={product.id} className="product-card">
          <img src={product.image} alt={product.title} />
          <h3>{product.title}</h3>
          <p>${product.price}</p>
        </div>
      ))}
    </div>
  );
}

export default ProductList;
```

With this, you can see the images and the text!

A Personal Insight: I can't emphasize enough how important it is to read and understand what is the goal of the code, rather than just using what it is! With that in mind, it will be a lot easier to do what you want.

Congratulations and Keep Going!

10.5 Project 5: Weather App – Integrating APIs and Dynamic Updates: Predicting the Weather

You've made a store, and you have all the Javascript. What can you do to then have it be that much more amazing? Well, you can now make a weather app!

Let's make a weather application, where you can type in a city and then have the Javascript show you.

To create this, we will need to think about:

1. What is the weather API and how to connect to it?
2. What pieces and information do we use to connect to it?
3. How to use Javascript to then create all of those actions?

That is what is going to make this so much more useful and easier to think of.

A Personal Insight: I love using weather apps, so I was really excited to try and create one! I'd recommend you use some of the tips to make it look and to be effective!

Choosing a Weather API: Your Data Source

There are many weather APIs available, both free and paid. Some popular options include:

- OpenWeatherMap: (Requires an API key)
- WeatherAPI.com: (Offers a free tier with limited usage)
- AccuWeather: (Offers a free tier with limited usage)

For this example, we'll use OpenWeatherMap, as it's relatively easy to use and offers a free tier that is sufficient for our needs. You'll need to sign up for a free API key at https://openweathermap.org/.

You will see a lot of weird keys and code, but keep in mind that as long as you are following the instructions, it will be fine!

Here is the code for it all,

First, add the state! You will likely need:

- What's the current city.
- What's the data about the city?
- Is it loading?

This is the most basic you will need to have to make it all clear!

To make that code, you will need the following:

```
    const [city, setCity] = useState('');
  const [weatherData, setWeatherData] = useState(null);
  const [loading, setLoading] = useState(false);
  const [error, setError] = useState(null);
```

Then after that, what you have to do is make the code that does it and to save it.

A Personal Insight: Make sure to always test and not expect it to all work on the first try!

Put it all together and you get this!

```
    import React, { useState, useEffect } from 'react';

function WeatherApp() {
  const [city, setCity] = useState('');
  const [weatherData, setWeatherData] = useState(null);
  const [loading, setLoading] = useState(false);
  const [error, setError] = useState(null);

  const API_KEY = 'YOUR_OPENWEATHERMAP_API_KEY'; // Replace with your API key

  const fetchWeather = async () => {
    setLoading(true);
    setError(null);

    try {
      const response = await
fetch(`https://api.openweathermap.org/data/2.5/weather?q=${city}&appid=${API_
KEY}&units=metric`);
      if (!response.ok) {
        throw new Error(`HTTP error! status: ${response.status}`);
      }
      const data = await response.json();
      setWeatherData(data);
    } catch (error) {
      setError(error);
      setWeatherData(null);
    } finally {
      setLoading(false);
    }
  };

  const handleSubmit = (e) => {
    e.preventDefault();
    fetchWeather();
  };

  return (
    <div>
      <form onSubmit={handleSubmit}>
        <input
          type="text"
```

```
        value={city}
        onChange={(e) => setCity(e.target.value)}
        placeholder="Enter city name"
      />
      <button type="submit">Get Weather</button>
    </form>

    {loading && <p>Loading weather data...</p>}

    {error && <p>Error: {error.message}</p>}

    {weatherData && (
      <div>
        <h2>Weather in {weatherData.name}</h2>
        <p>Temperature: {weatherData.main.temp}°C</p>
        <p>Description: {weatherData.weather[0].description}</p>
      </div>
    )}
    </div>
  );
}

export default WeatherApp;
```

All of it in one! You see this Javascript code, and hopefully you can understand all the different parts that you can use! With this, you can see all the great things that Javascript can do.

Congratulations! You've completed a series of mini-projects that have put your React skills to the test. You are now more than capable of starting and building what you have learned! What now is to use this knowledge to grow!

These are all the skills that are essential to get to the end of this book! It is time to say goodbye!

Conclusion: Your React.js Journey and Beyond – From Beginner to Builder

Congratulations! You've reached the end of this React.js Crash Course. You've journeyed from the fundamentals of components and JSX to the power of state management, event handling, and data fetching. You've even built a collection of mini-projects to showcase your new skills.

But remember, this is just the beginning! The world of React is vast and constantly evolving, and there's always something new to learn. This conclusion provides a roadmap for your next steps, pointing you towards key takeaways, resources for continued learning, and a glimpse into the future of React development.

- **Key Takeaways and Best Practices:**
  - **Components are King:** Master the art of breaking down your UI into reusable components.
  - **State is Your Friend:** Use state to make your components dynamic and interactive.
  - **Hooks are Powerful:** Leverage Hooks to manage state, side effects, and reusable logic in functional components.
  - **Data Fetching is Essential:** Know how to fetch data from APIs and display it in your components.
  - **Structure Matters:** Organize your project and components for better maintainability.
  - **Testing is Crucial:** Write tests to ensure the quality and reliability of your code.
- **Resources for Continued Learning and Community Engagement:**
  - **The Official React Documentation:** https://reactjs.org/ – Your definitive source for all things React.
  - **React Tutorial:** https://reactjs.org/tutorial/tutorial.html – A great way to reinforce your understanding of the fundamentals.
  - **Stack Overflow:** https://stackoverflow.com/questions/tagged/reactjs – The best place to find answers to your React questions.
  - **React Communities on Reddit (r/reactjs):** https://www.reddit.com/r/reactjs/ – Engage with other React developers, ask questions, and share your projects.
  - **Online Courses (Udemy, Coursera, freeCodeCamp):** Explore in-depth courses on React and related technologies.
- **The Future of React: A Dynamic Landscape:**

  The React ecosystem is constantly evolving, with new features, libraries, and tools emerging all the time. Here are a few trends to watch out for:

  - **Server Components:** A new feature in React 18 that allows you to render components on the server, improving performance and SEO.
  - **TypeScript:** Using TypeScript with React can improve code quality and maintainability by adding static typing.

- **Meta-Frameworks (Next.js, Remix):** These frameworks build upon React to provide features like server-side rendering, routing, and API endpoints, making it easier to build full-stack applications.

Appendix A: React Cheat Sheet: JSX, Hooks, and Common Patterns

[This appendix would provide a quick reference guide to React syntax, including:]

- **JSX:**
  - Basic syntax: <element>
  - Embedding JavaScript expressions: {expression}
  - Conditional rendering: {condition ? <ComponentA /> : <ComponentB />}
  - Rendering lists: array.map(item => <Component key={item.id} item={item} />)
- **Hooks:**
  - useState: const [state, setState] = useState(initialValue);
  - useEffect: useEffect(() => { /* side effect */ }, [dependencies]);
  - useContext: const value = useContext(MyContext);
  - useReducer: const [state, dispatch] = useReducer(reducer, initialState);
- **Common Patterns:**
  - Controlled Components: Linking input values to component state.
  - Event Handling: onClick, onChange, onSubmit

Appendix B: Setting Up Your Development Environment (VS Code, etc.)

[This appendix would provide detailed, step-by-step instructions for setting up a React development environment using VS Code, including:]

- Installing Node.js and npm (or yarn)
- Installing VS Code
- Installing helpful VS Code extensions (e.g., ESLint, Prettier)
- Creating a new React project using Create React App
- Running the development server

Glossary of React Terms

[This appendix defines key React terms:]

- **Component:** A reusable building block of a React user interface.
- **DOM (Document Object Model):** The tree-like representation of an HTML document.
- **JSX (JavaScript XML):** A syntax extension to JavaScript that allows you to write HTML-like code within your JavaScript files.
- **Props (Properties):** Data that is passed from a parent component to a child component.
- **State:** Data that is managed within a component and can change over time.
- **Hook:** A function that lets you "hook into" React state and lifecycle features from functional components.

- **useEffect:** A Hook that lets you perform side effects in functional components.
- **Context API:** A way to share data between components without having to pass props manually at every level.